COLLEGE
WITH
NO REGRETS

COLLEGE
WITH
NO REGRETS

Wisdom for the Journey

RICHARD E. SIMMONS III

Union Hill Publishing
200 Union Hill Drive, Suite 200
Birmingham, AL 35209

www.richardsimmons3.org

1 2 3 4 5 6 7 8 9 10

Printed in the United States of America

TABLE OF CONTENTS

INTRODUCTION

··

Whether you're in college, or about to enter college, this book is for you.

College is one of the most exciting and meaningful times in life. You make new friends, many of whom will last a lifetime. You experience new freedoms: no curfews, chores, or asking your parents for permission to go places. However, for all the exciting things college offers, I'm sure you're also wrestling with some big questions—perhaps even some fear or anxiety. Who am I? Will I succeed academically? What do I really believe?

College is a season of transition. You've likely moved out of your parents' house (or another guardian), and now face decisions independently, apart from their positive influence. For some of you, home life has been more hurtful than helpful, and you're happy to leave it in the rear view. College is a first step into adulthood, allowing you to make a lot of your own choices. These next four years (at least) will pass by quickly, so ask yourself, "What do I hope life will look like when I get out of college? Am I prepared to face the real world on my own?"

One key thing separates an unfulfilling college experience from a life-changing one: the choices you make. These choices will ultimately determine whether you thrive in college or it ends up being a major disappointment. The best way to prepare yourself to make these crucial decisions is to think through them now.

As someone who navigated the college season myself, and who has helped guide my three kids through it, I've written this book to help you prepare for what lies ahead. Without question the truths I share here have made a significant difference in my own life. My hope is that this book will make you wiser and equip you to better navigate your own journey through the college experience.

I'd love to hear from you!

Email me at richard@richardesimmons3.com

—*Richard E. Simmons III*

CHAPTER 1

WISDOM FOR
THE JOURNEY

1.1

The Path of Wisdom

I f you could change one thing about your college experience, what would it be? That's the exact question Dr. Richard Light, Professor of Teaching at Harvard Graduate School of Education, poses to his students every semester. He summarizes their responses in a *New York Times* article titled, "How to Live Wisely":

> Imagine you are dean for a day. What is one actionable change you would implement to enhance the college experience on campus? I have asked students this question for years. The answers can be eye-opening. A few years ago, the responses began to move away from "tweak the history course" or "change the way labs are structured." A different commentary, about learning to live wisely, has emerged.

Many people today are beginning to realize their current approach to life isn't working, including college students. They recognize that they're not living wisely, and they want to learn how. They're searching for a better way.

Wisdom is one of the greatest gifts God gives to any person. But before you can learn to live wisely, you need to understand the basic meaning of wisdom. The word "wisdom" comes from the Hebrew word *chokmah*, which means "to have skill or expertise in living." Wisdom gives us the ability to see things as they really are, not just as they appear to be. How you see the world determines how you live in it. If your vision is murky, you'll struggle to distinguish between what ideas are true and what ideas are false. Wisdom gives you the ability to see clearly.

Author Stephen Covey suggests that if people are going to lead healthy lives, their ideas about life must be rooted in what is true. He shares a wonderful illustration that demonstrates the importance of this truth:

> Suppose you wanted to arrive at a specific location in central Chicago. A street map of the city would be a great help to you in reaching your destination. But suppose you were given the wrong map. Through a printing error, the map labeled "Chicago" was actually a map of Detroit. Can you imagine the frustration, the ineffectiveness of trying to reach your destination?
>
> You might work on your behavior—you could try harder, be more diligent, double your speed. But your efforts would only succeed in getting you to the wrong place faster.
>
> You might work on your attitude—you could think more positively. You still wouldn't get to the right place, but perhaps you wouldn't care. Your attitude would be so positive, you'd be happy wherever you were.
>
> The point is, you'd still be lost. The fundamental problem has nothing to do with your behavior or your attitude. It has everything to do with having the wrong map.
>
> If you have the right map of Chicago, then diligence becomes important, and when you encounter frustrat-

ing obstacles along the way, then attitude can make a real difference. But the first and most important requirement is the accuracy of the map.

As a college student, hold on to this helpful image. Many attempt to live their lives with maps that are wildly inaccurate. They have false ideas about life, success, identity and happiness. They don't realize they're making potentially life-altering decisions every day based on these false maps (false ideas) that they have mentally developed throughout their lives. Can you imagine how frustrating it would be to look up one day and realize you've been making directional decisions during your college years based on a faulty map? How devastating to waste all that time, make all those wrong turns, and to feel so disoriented.

French mathematician and philosopher Blaise Pascal, one of the most brilliant men to ever live, recognized that all human beings are on a quest for happiness, but most never attain it. He strongly believed that unhappiness is a symptom of false ideas, and that true happiness can only be found by uprooting false beliefs and replacing them with genuine wisdom.

The Age of Information Overload

Today's world is flooded with information. Many people are convinced that knowledge is the key to success. Yet, every day we read of highly educated fools who ruin their lives through bad decisions. For example, you can read all the dating advice in the world, but lack the courage to walk up to the guy or girl that you'd like to introduce yourself to. Apart from wisdom, information stays in your head but never benefits your life. Sometimes it's the *most* knowledgeable people who lack wisdom. It's not the *quantity* of what we know that matters most; it's the *quality* of our knowledge that makes a difference.

Unfortunately, the pace of today's society leaves little room for wisdom. For most of us, the distractions and frantic nature of the digital world do not encourage deep thought, reflection, or introspection.

Some people assume wisdom is mainly about making good moral choices. If they do the right things, life will go well. It's true that bad moral choices can destroy your life, but life is more complex than a simple formula of cause-and-effect. Wisdom allows us to see nuance and take many things into consideration when we make decisions. "Right living" is about much more than just being moral or good.

Wisdom helps you make choices that aren't necessarily good or bad, right or wrong. Most of the choices and decisions we make are not moral ones. As a college student, here's some pivotal (but non-moral) decisions you're likely to face:

- ➢ Where should I go to college?
- ➢ What should I major in?
- ➢ Should I take out a student loan?
- ➢ Should I be in a fraternity or sorority?
- ➢ Who should I spend time with?
- ➢ How should I spend my time?
- ➢ What are my priorities?

Wisdom provides insight into the true nature of things—both physical and spiritual reality. It allows us to grow in competence as we respond to the realities of life with the bigger picture in mind. Wisdom is knowing how things truly work and why things happen, and then knowing what to do about it. This is why Solomon tells us wisdom is more valuable than silver and gold—that nothing we desire compares with it. As a college student, it is the key to living well.

Questions for Reflection

1. Do you think your map (ideas about reality) is accurate or inaccurate? How do you know?

2. In an age of excessive information, how can you discern what's helpful and what's just noise?

3. What are 1–2 big decisions facing you right now that require wisdom? Have you asked God to grant you wisdom for these decisions?

The Value of Wisdom

Have you ever known someone who makes one bad decision after another until their life comes crashing down around them? Unfortunately this happens to college students a lot. Without the protection of wisdom, the exciting possibilities of college can turn into devastating catastrophes.

Wisdom allows us to understand the laws and principles of life—to live in reality. Years ago, I read this simple illustration of how wisdom works in our lives:

A little girl watches her mother ironing clothes. The child is intrigued by the process as the iron eats up the wrinkles and creases in each garment. The phone rings. As the mother goes to answer it, she says to her little girl, "Don't touch that iron; it's hot." The child now has knowledge—the iron is hot. As soon as her mother disappears, the little girl decides to try her own hand at ironing. Unfortunately, she touches the iron in the wrong place and is burned. She now has understanding—the iron is hot. The next day the mother continues with the ironing and again she is summoned by the phone. Once again, she issues a warning: "Don't touch the iron; it's hot." The temptation to iron clothes comes over the little girl. She puts out her hand to grab the iron. Then she remembers her burned finger and leaves the iron alone. She now has wisdom—the iron is hot.

The illustration shows how wisdom impacts the choices we make. When you get right down to it, wisdom changes people. It impacts how you see the world around you. Your choices determine the ultimate outcome of your life, so choose wisely.

While it's fun to live in the moment, wise people think ahead. They understand that all of life is connected. There is a cause-and-effect relationship between the choices one makes today and what one experiences tomorrow. If you have a midterm on Friday morning, you may want to skip the party on Thursday. If you know someone doesn't share your faith or values, wisdom says that, even though you find them attractive, best to move on.

In Proverbs 27:12, Solomon says: "A prudent man sees evil and hides himself, but the naïve proceed and pay the penalty." Commenting on this verse, author Andy Stanley says:

Prudent people look as far down the road as possible when making decisions. Every decision. After all, they understand that today and tomorrow are connected. As the author of Proverbs states, they stay on the lookout for signs of trouble up ahead. Today's decisions are informed and influenced by their impact on tomorrow. Drawing on their own experience and the experience of others, they anticipate the future and choose accordingly. They ask, "In light of my past experience and my future hopes and dreams, what's the wise thing to do?" The prudent draw upon the wealth of data that life has already provided them and take appropriate action when they see danger ahead.

In contrast to the prudent, the simple or naïve person lives as though life is disconnected, as if there is no connection between today's choices and tomorrow's experiences. When the simple "see danger," they don't take evasive action. They keep going.

Notice, I said they live as if life is disconnected. They don't necessarily believe that to be the case. If you were to ask them, "Do you think there is a connection between the choices you make today and what you will experience in the future?" they would probably answer, "Yes." Again, it is not that they don't believe life is connected. The point is they don't live as if it is.

The 1960's are a helpful example of how unwise decisions can lead to disaster. It was a turbulent time in our country when many college students despised the structure they witnessed in the lives of their parents. They longed to be liberated from the restrictions mainstream culture imposed upon them. Many of them dropped out of college and lived in communes.

In the Haight-Ashbury District of San Francisco, a group of hippies decided that hygiene was a middle-class hang-up they could do without. They chose to live without baths or showers. Novelist Tom Wolfe was intrigued by these hippies, who "sought nothing less than to sweep aside all codes and restraints of the past and start out from zero." They aspired to be totally autonomous and free.

Before long, the hippies' aversion to modern hygiene yielded unpleasant consequences they had not considered. Wolfe explains:

At the Haight-Ashbury Free Clinic, there were doctors who were treating diseases no living doctor had ever encountered before, diseases that had disappeared so long ago that they had never even picked up Latin names, such as the mange, the grunge, the scroff, and the rot. The itching and the mange began to vex these hippies, leading them to seek help from the local free clinics. Step by step, they were forced to rediscover for themselves the necessity of modern hygiene.

As these hygiene-defying hippies discovered, there are certain universal principles built into life, and we violate them at our own risk. Wisdom not only respects this underlying structure, but lives by it. This is why Solomon says, "Wisdom preserves the lives of its possessors." (Ecclesiastes 7:12)

College is a great place to put wisdom into practice. The question is, will you do it?

Questions for Reflection

1. Do you tend to live for the moment, or do you prefer to plan ahead? What are the pros and cons of your personality?

2. In your opinion, what are some of the biggest mistakes students make during their college career—mistakes that end up sabotaging their future? How can you avoid those mistakes?

3. As a college student, what kinds of decisions can you make today that will benefit you in ten years?

1.3

·········

The Key to a Healthy Life

Healthy people are happy people. The problem is, many people are trying to be happy without first being healthy. College students are no exception. They struggle to cope with life in a season filled with changes and challenges.

What does it mean to be "healthy?" Being healthy means that our mental, emotional, psychological and spiritual selves are aligned with God's wisdom.

Dr. Scott Peck gives great insight into this issue in his bestselling book, *The Road Less Traveled.* His opening words in the book are, "Life is difficult." Dr. Peck explains that life is a series of problems. We have two options: we can complain and ignore our problems, or we can try to solve them. Confronting our problems head-on can be painful. However, Dr. Peck believes the process of facing and solving problems is key to achieving mental and spiritual health. He then shares what he believes is the key to becoming a healthy person. Dr. Peck calls it "being dedicated to the truth." He says:

> The less clearly we see the reality of the world—the more our minds are befuddled by falsehood, misperceptions and illusions—the less able we will be to

determine correct courses of action and make wise decisions.

In his book, *12 Rules for Life*, psychologist Jordan Peterson similarly argues that, if you want real chaos in your life, don't deal with your problems. Let them linger, ignore them, pretend like they aren't there.

Sometimes we believe that ignoring our issues will make them go away. But problems aren't so easily ditched. It's easy to assume (naively) that most challenges self-resolve, but in reality time only makes them worse. Like mold, they spread and grow. They get bigger.

Peterson cites the children's story, *There's No Such Thing as a Dragon*, by Jack Kent, to teach this valuable lesson.

It's about a small boy, Billy Bixbee, who spies a dragon sitting on his bed one morning. It's about the size of a house cat, and friendly. He tells his mother about it, but she tells him there's no such thing as a dragon. So, it starts to grow. It eats all of Billy's pancakes. Soon it fills the whole house. Mom tries to vacuum, but she has to go in and out of the house through the windows because of the dragon everywhere. It takes her forever. Then, the dragon runs off with the house. Billy's dad comes home – and there's just an empty space, where he used to live. The mailman tells him where the house went. He chases after it, climbs up the dragon's head and neck (now sprawling out into the street) and rejoins his wife and son. Mom still insists that the dragon does not exist, but Billy, who's pretty much had it by now, insists, "There is a dragon, Mom." Instantly, it starts to shrink. Soon, it's cat-sized again. Everyone agrees that dragons of that size (1) exist and (2) are much preferable to their giant counterparts. Mom, eyes reluctantly opened by this point, asks somewhat plaintively why it had to get so big. Billy quietly suggests: "Maybe it wanted to be noticed."

Peterson says when we sweep our problems under the rug, we're actually feeding our dragon. One day, that dragon will burst forth in a way that you can no longer ignore. The result is usually chaos and misery.

So, examine your life and ask: *Where are the dragons in my life?*

- Am I healthy mentally, emotionally and spiritually?

- Are my friendships healthy?

- Are there things I'm hiding from the people closest to me?

- What destructive habits do I have in my life? How much time do I give to social media? Netflix? YouTube?

- Am I growing and developing as a person? Do I have older mentors who regularly speak into my life? Am I pouring into someone younger than me?

- Do I have problems that I'm afraid to confront? Am I addicted to pornography?

- Do I eat healthy meals? Do I overeat? Undereat?

- What is the state of my relationship with God? Am I connected to a local church, or am I trying to follow God alone?

Are you willing to look reality in the eye and then act upon what you know to be true? How badly do you want to be a healthy person? Unfortunately, many people delude themselves into believing that everything will eventually work out. Instead of action, they do nothing. If you want to be healthy, run towards your problems, not away from them! College is bound to throw some challenges your way. But armed with God's wisdom, you can confront them head-on and thrive.

Questions for Reflection

1. Do you tend to face your problems or ignore them?

   ....

   ....

2. Is there a problem in your life you've been avoiding? What is one tangible thing you can do today to face this problem head-on?

   ....

   ....

   ....

   ....

3. Who is a trusted person in your life who can help, encourage, and support you as you confront your problems? Have you reached out to them yet?

   ....

   ....

CHAPTER 2

LIVING AN EXCEPTIONAL LIFE

The Life That Could Have Been

For many people, there's often a massive gap between the life they dream about in college and the life they end up living. That gap, between their dream and reality, can be so disappointing. Why is this letdown so common?

In the long-run, wisdom offers the longest lasting, most satisfying pleasure. Yet we are often guided by our feelings and emotions instead of wise judgment. In those situations, we prioritize temporary pleasure over what will be most beneficial to us in the future.

An analogous parallel would be fast food. It gives you a quick, tasty, sodium-loaded fix, but fails to nourish. On the other hand, eating healthier, home-cooked meals makes you vibrant and stronger in the long run.

Research reveals that many adults are like children when it comes to instant gratification. If you offer a child the choice between a slice of cake now or a $10,000 scholarship for college later, he'll almost *always* choose the cake. Children invariably choose short-term thrills over long-term benefits. They don't understand the value of delayed gratification, and many adults are no different. They almost always choose temporary, feel-good pleasures over what has lasting value.

The human heart, with all its conflicting desires, is difficult to understand. Have you ever noticed how contradictory your desires can be? For example, you might enjoy the rush of partying all night with friends on a weeknight, while simultaneously aspiring to excel academically. You're likely to face all sorts of conflicting desires during college:

- Living an undistracted life vs. consuming hours of social media every day
- Sleeping in on Sundays vs. serving at a local church
- Wanting a lasting relationship vs. settling for dates with people you know aren't right for you
- Desiring independence vs. receiving support from your parents
- Embracing sexual integrity vs. seeking the adrenaline rush of sexual experimentation
- Wanting to build a career vs. wanting to hang out with friends
- Doing something we love that pays modestly vs. doing something we dislike that pays great

Our desires often conflict with one another. Like a Door-Dash delivery, we want dopamine dropped into our lives quickly and conveniently. Wisdom, however, recognizes the importance of discovering which desires are beneficial and which are destructive. Wisdom refuses to cave to every urge, but considers whether or not a particular desire aligns with one's identity and goals.

Oscar Wilde, the Irish author and poet, is one of the most gifted writers who ever lived. He was educated in some of Great Britain's finest schools and excelled in the Greek language. His writing earned him great wealth, and he was the pride of London. One literary critic described him as "our most quotable writer" after Shakespeare. Sadly, however, Wilde squandered all he had and died penniless. Before he died, he reflected on his life and penned these words:

> I must say to myself that I ruined myself, and that nobody great or small can be ruined except by his own hand... Terrible as what the world did to me, what I did to myself was far more terrible still.
>
> The gods had given me almost everything. But I let myself be lured into long spells of senseless and sensual ease. I surrounded myself with the smaller natures and the meaner minds. I became the spendthrift of my own genius, and to waste an eternal youth gave me a curious joy.
>
> Tired of being on the heights, I deliberately went to the depths in search for new sensation. What the paradox was to me in the sphere of thought, perversity became to me in the sphere of passion. Desire, at the end, was a malady, or a madness, or both. I grew careless of the lives of others. I took pleasure where it pleased me, and passed on. *I forgot that every little action of the common day makes or unmakes character, and that therefore what one has done in the secret chamber one has some day to cry aloud on the housetop.* I ceased to be lord over myself. I was no longer the captain of my soul, and did not know it.

Wilde desired to live a long life and produce great literary work, but he also loved pleasure. In the end, as he put it himself, "I allowed pleasure to dominate me. I ended in horrible disgrace." Wilde died a broken man at the age of forty-six. His life potently illustrates that even with great success, taking the easy path to pleasure can tear it all down.

One of our family's mottos comes from the book *Do Hard Things*. As I tell my children, the path that leads to excellence is often harder than the path that leads to instant gratification. But as we persist down that difficult path, it becomes easier. This isn't because the task has become less challenging, but because our ability to do it has grown.

My wife Holly provides a good example of this. Though she didn't grow up swimming, several years ago she challenged herself to become a better swimmer. The first time she swam laps in the pool, she swallowed a good bit of water. Needless to say, there was nothing enjoyable about the experience. But she stuck with it, and over time her swimming improved. Difficult workouts became easier. Now Holly no longer dreads the pool—she enjoys it! And she reaps the many benefits that come from swimming.

Author and pastor John Piper was correct when he said:

All training is painful and frustrating as you seek to develop certain skills. However, over time, as these skills become second nature, they lead to greater joy.

If you invest time each day in important activities and skill development, you'll eventually become very capable. What skills or habits do you hope to develop in your college years? Here are a few examples:

- Read the Bible every day
- Work out several times a week
- Cook your own meals

- Play a musical instrument
- Learn to write code
- Become a better writer or speaker
- Become a better friend
- Start a business

Repetition is the key to enhancing your skills. With persistence, you can develop habits and disciplines that lead to an exceptional life. As you make small-but-wise investments day by day, you'll slowly see growth. The life that "could have been" becomes the "life that is."

Questions for Reflection

1. Are you more guided by feelings or logic? How can you become more balanced?

   ....
   ....

2. Have you ever experienced the benefits of delaying gratification in order to get something better? How did that experience shape your perspective on life?

   ....
   ....
   ....

3. What is one thing you can invest small amounts of time in now, in order to reach a desired goal down the road? How can you start pursuing that goal today?

   ....
   ....
   ....
   ....

2.2

....

The Art of Achieving

What makes some people succeed and others fail? In his book *Flourish*, psychologist Dr. Martin Seligman suggests that growth in any area of life is directly related to the amount of skill you have, multiplied by the effort you expend. He defines effort as the time you are willing to spend on a task.

Seligman references the findings of Dr. Anders Ericsson, an internationally renowned psychologist who argues that the greatest experts excel through deliberate practice, not God-given genius. Mozart distinguished himself not primarily because he was a naturally gifted musician, but because he spent all of his time honing his gift from toddlerhood on. World-class chess players don't think faster than novice players because they have higher IQs. They're speedy because they've been playing for years, and over time, their skills grew.

Many people desire excellence in a field or craft, but as Dr. Seligman points out, it takes character to put in the time needed to excel. In other words, what you devote time to shows who you are. Self-discipline—the ability to make yourself do something you don't necessarily want to do—eventually produces the result you want to see.

Seligman also shares interesting research on self-discipline from a study of the students of Masterman High School in Philadelphia. Masterman accepts promising students beginning in the fifth grade, but due to the school's rigorous academics, many students drop out before they reach ninth grade. Researchers studied a group of Masterman's eighth graders to gauge whether their success was a result of IQ or self-discipline.

They employed a battery of tests to determine which students possessed the character trait of self-discipline. For instance, students were tested on their ability to delay gratification through questions like: "Would you rather receive five dollars today or ten dollars in two weeks?" This study revealed some striking traits in these eighth graders, including:

- Higher grade point averages
- Higher achievement test scores
- Spent more time on homework and started it earlier in the day
- Had better attendance
- Watched less television

In the end, their research concluded that self-discipline is two times more likely to produce academic success than a high IQ. When people underachieve in any area of life, they often look for something or someone to blame. But the *real* reason they underachieve is their unwillingness to sacrifice short-term pleasure for long-term gain. As you enter college to pursue your goals, many forms of instant gratification await you. Are you willing to be self-disciplined to push them aside in order to get what you want *most?*

Questions For Reflection

1. What skill(s) or knowledge have you developed through years of intentional practice? What skill(s) do you want to improve in?

2. Have you ever given up after starting to pursue a goal or learn a new skill? What did you learn from that experience?

3. What is one simple way you can delay gratification today, in order to build more resilience? Who can support you in this challenge?

2.3

....

Disordered Priorities

What is your latest obsession? Is it the famous-for-being-famous celebrity you're following on social media? Or maybe it's this week's winning lineup for Fantasy football?

Dr. Armand Nicholi was a professor who used to teach at Harvard Medical School. As he explained in an interview, each semester he liked to ask his students the same question:

> I teach people who are just starting out. As Harvard students, they're all bright to start with, and they often have talents or interests that they're actively pursuing. But, early in the semester I ask them, "What is your goal in life?" Invariably they answer, "To be successful." So, I ask, "What does that mean to you?" Their answer has some relationship to fame and fortune.

After listening to their predictable answers, Dr. Nicholi would reframe the question:

> I tell them we all have a lifespan of about 30,000 days... and we spend about a third of that time sleeping. That

means we have a waking lifespan of about 20,000 days. Then I say, 'If you had 20 days left, what would you do with them?' They universally answer that they would spend that time working on their relationships with family and friends, and if they're people of faith, with their God.

Dr. Nicholi realized that his students' obsession with fame and fortune conflicted with their highest stated priority: friends and family. Despite his advice, most of Dr. Nicholi's students still prioritized wealth over their spouses, and settled for superficial relationships with their children. In Dr. Nicholi's words, they had "disordered priorities."

It's tragic that our desire for fame, wealth and glory can blind us to what really matters. C.S. Lewis warns about this same blindness in his renowned speech, "The Inner Ring," which he delivered at King's College. He warns them about the folly of seeking acceptance in elite inner circles. These cliques, Lewis explains, inevitably form and reform, coming and going throughout a person's life. They lack stability and provide only superficial friendship.

The ambition to be an insider—to cozy up to those who are important and well-to-do, can consume you. According to Lewis, chasing acceptance is as futile as staggering toward a mirage in the desert. Ultimately, your quest to be in the inner circle of the powerful will leave you parched, desperate for meaningful relationships. As you walk through your college experience, there will be many voices telling you the most important priority in life is your paycheck. How will you protect your heart, and most importantly, your closest relationships?

Questions for Reflection

1. What is your goal in life? If someone were to observe your life and habits, would this goal be obvious?

   ....
   ....

2. How important are the relationships in your life? Do you agree with Dr. Nicholi's students, that relationships are the most important thing?

   ....
   ....

3. How can you guard your life from the vain pursuit of wealth, fame, and glory? How is your life centered around God's glory?

   ....
   ....
   ....
   ....

2.4
....

Understanding Our Habits

Do you have any bad habits in your life that you can't seem to break? I don't know anyone who intentionally forms bad habits—they tend to develop silently over time. By the time we notice them, they've already gained a foothold in our daily lives.

Dr. Tom Morris, a professor of philosophy at Notre Dame, says:

> Good habits usually result from thoughtful, rational decision-making plus personal discipline and repetition. When establishing a new habit, getting started is generally the hardest part.
>
> Bad habits, on the other hand, are usually not the result of logical thought or careful deliberation. Frequently, they are a result of pleasurable sensations that make us feel good. And if it results in making us feel better, then we are prone to doing it again and again. Repetition sets in and behold—a new habit has formed.

Over the years, I've wondered why people develop such destructive patterns in their lives. Why would anyone embrace something guaranteed to eventually harm them?

Recently I had an aha moment while reading some profound words by author James Clear. He says we value the present more than we value the future. We prefer instant gratification over delayed gratification. He asks: Why smoke if it dramatically increases the risk of lung cancer? Why overeat when it increases the risk of obesity and heart disease? The reason is clear: *The consequences of bad habits are delayed, while the rewards are immediate.*

Think about it. Smoking might kill you in ten years, but it reduces stress and eases nicotine cravings now. Overeating is ultimately harmful, though it's satisfying in the moment. With our bad habits, the immediate outcome usually feels good, but the ultimate outcome feels bad. Conversely, good habits start as unenjoyable, but ultimately satisfy. The French economist Frédéric Bastiat explains the problem clearly when he writes:

> It almost always happens that when the immediate consequence is favorable, the later consequences are disastrous, and vice versa . . . Often, the sweeter the first fruit of a habit, the more bitter are its later fruits.

The bottom line is, you pay the price for your good habits *now*. You will pay the price for your bad habits *later*. Wise people think ahead. They understand that there is a cause-and-effect relationship between the choices we make today and the life we will live tomorrow.

Questions for Reflection

1. Where are you tempted to let feelings overcome common sense? How can you counteract that tendency?

2. Are you aware of any bad habits that have silently crept into your life? What are they, and how can you work toward healthier habits?

3. As you think about your bad habits, what are the "immediate rewards" that keep you engaged in them? What better rewards are available, down the road, if you break these bad habits?

The Power of Discipline

What do you want in life? The way you answer that question says a lot about you. The book of Proverbs has much to say about the importance of controlling our desires and appetites. While God has created us with strong desires (this is good), sin distorts our desires so that they end up controlling us.

In Proverbs 25:28, Solomon says, "Like a city where walls are broken down is a man who lacks self-control." In ancient times, a city without walls was a disaster waiting to happen. Walls around a community gave it security and enabled it to flourish. Without them, everyone was vulnerable to attack.

Like an ancient city wall, discipline is a protective buffer from unhelpful desires, as pastor Andy Stanley explains:

Our desires and appetites bring zest and passion to life. But they are terrible filters for making decisions. Clearly it is not an exaggeration to say that your response to your appetites will determine the direction and quality of your life. You've certainly seen friends and family members wreck their lives over their seeming inability to say no to themselves.

If you want to be a person of character, you must have the ability to restrain your desires and deny your will. A well-disciplined person knows how to forfeit a momentary desire for something more valuable. Discipline is a form of wisdom. It's the ability to choose the meaningful things in life over the momentary things.

If you lack discipline, your desires become disproportioned—what matters most gets eclipsed by what matters less. Many people's lives eventually fall apart because of a lack of discipline. They become like a city without walls, defenseless against the chaos that ultimately overruns their lives. Unfortunately, I have seen this play out in my life.

When I started my career after college, I was not very disciplined. I would work all day, sometimes I might exercise, some days I wouldn't. I watched television, I would read a little and go to bed later than I should have. I would get up just in time to make it to work.

Then one evening I read some words that would change the trajectory of my life. It was the biography of John Wesley, founder of the Methodist Church. At a certain point in his life he came to the realization that if he was to be the man God desired him to be, he must be willing to walk down a different path than other men. Wesley decided to start by getting up at 5:00 a.m. each day.

That day I made the decision to change the habits in my life. During the work week I would get up at 5:00 a.m. I now had three hours to use productively before getting ready for work. I would read the Bible, pray, workout and read *The Wall Street Journal*. Here I am 44 years later and I can say that one changed habit has had the greatest impact on my life.

Over forty years ago, I read a short magazine article that impacted me. It's titled "Discipline," and I still read it from time to time as a reminder.

We conquer outer space and body-devastating diseases and apply ourselves to finding alternative fuel sources, but there is a frontier, a mountain called discipline, that many have never conquered. Some have never even tried to conquer it.

If drug abuse, alcoholism and other "escapes" are some people's response to pain or anything else that is disagreeable, then so are the many others in our Western world. There is a weakness, a basic unwillingness, to cope with unpleasantness or difficulty, and inability to endure, and we see it everywhere. Some call it the freedom to be, but it isn't freedom. Lack of discipline is slavery.

When I cannot or will not say "no," I offer myself to be shackled by any impulse, yearning or fleeting pleasure that comes along. When I allow myself to be directed by whatever is easy or promises immediate gratification, I am as incapable of standing as a rootless tree.

When I trade duty for pleasure, honor for expediency, God's call for my wants, I deal in the business of human failure.

Temptations come; of course, they do. Situations present themselves, escape from emotional or physical unpleasantness is attractive, the broad path offers fewer obstacles. But strength comes in the moral and spiritual muscle-building that demands effort, even strain—it is a pushing-against or a pulling-back.

When you walk onto your college campus, discipline will be rare. Momentary thrills will be the popular choice. But if you embrace wisdom now, your life will truly stand out. Be willing to walk down the road less traveled. We need disciplined men and women and their examples on our college campuses now more than ever.

In the end, the decisive question isn't: What do I want in life? Ask instead: How do I manage my desires—intentionally or impulsively?

Questions for Reflection

1. Does the word "discipline" evoke a positive or negative response in you? Why?

2. Can you think of a time when discipline (restraining your desires) proved helpful?

3. Who is someone you love or respect, who models a life of healthy discipline? How can you emulate their habits?

2.6

....

The Daffodil Principle

I'm convinced that an exceptional life is determined by how wisely we invest our time.

In his book, *The Best Question Ever,* author Andy Stanley points out the cumulative value of investing small amounts of time in something over the long haul. Notice those two words: *cumulative value.*

Cumulative value applies to every area of your life. For example, if you exercise 35 to 45 minutes a day, five days a week, over a 40-year period, the cumulative effect is a healthy body. Conversely, if you sit on the couch and binge-watch Netflix every day, you'll probably be out of shape.

When you invest consistent, incremental effort into something, it makes a lasting difference. It's the difference between a single workout vs. a lifetime of workouts. Exercise has a compounding effect. The same principle applies with investing in your relationships. Relationships can provide the necessary emotional support to help a student cope with the pressures of school.

Cumulative value also impacts your finances. Albert Einstein said, "Compound interest is the most powerful force in the universe."

In Darren Hardy's book *The Compound Effect*, he shares the illustration of the magic penny.

If you were given the choice of receiving $3 million in cash right now or a single penny that would double in value every day for 31 days, which would you choose? Most people impulsively choose the $3 million in cash. But if you chose the penny, on Day 5 you would have 16 cents, and on Day 10, $5.12. After 20 days, with only 11 left, you would have $5,243. This is when the power of compounding begins its rapid increase. On Day 31, you would have $10,737,418.24!

Pennies seem so insignificant, but with time, they can turn into a fortune. This same compounding force exists in every area of life. The cumulative effect of investing small amounts of time in carefully chosen activities over a long period is powerfully explained in *The Daffodil Principle*, a book by Jaroldeen Edwards:

Several times my daughter had telephoned to say, "Mother, you must come see the daffodils before they are over." I wanted to go, but it was a two-hour drive from Laguna to Lake Arrowhead. "I will come next Tuesday," I promised, a little reluctantly, on her third call.

Next Tuesday dawned cold and rainy. Still, I had promised, and so I drove there. When I finally walked into Carolyn's house and hugged and greeted my grandchildren, I said, "Forget the daffodils, Carolyn! The road is invisible in the clouds and fog, and there is nothing in the world except you and these children that I want to see bad enough to drive another inch!" My daughter smiled calmly and said, "We drive in this all the time, Mother."

"Well, you won't get me back on the road until it clears, and then I'm heading home!" I assured her.

"I was hoping you'd take me to the garage to pick up my car."

"How far will we have to drive?"

"Just a few blocks," Carolyn said. "I'll drive. I'm used to this."

After several minutes, I had to ask, "Where are we going? This isn't the way to the garage!"

"We're going to my garage the long way," Carolyn smiled, "by way of the daffodils."

"Carolyn," I said sternly, "please turn around."

"It's all right, Mother, I promise. You will never forgive yourself if you miss this experience."

After about 20 minutes, we turned onto a small gravel road and I saw a small church. On the far side of the church, I saw a hand-lettered sign with an arrow that read, Daffodil Garden. We got out of the car and each took a child's hand, and I followed Carolyn down the path. Then, we turned a corner of the path, and I looked up and gasped. Before me lay the most glorious sight.

It looked as though someone had taken a great vat of gold and poured it over the mountain peak and its surrounding slopes. The flowers were planted in majestic, swirling patterns—great ribbons and swaths of deep orange, white, lemon yellow, salmon pink, saffron and butter yellow. Each different-colored variety was planted as a group so that it swirled and flowed like its own river with its own unique hue.

There were five acres of flowers. "But who has done it?" I asked Carolyn. "It's just one woman," Carolyn answered. "She lives on the property. That's her home." Carolyn pointed to a well-kept A-frame house that looked small and modest in the midst of all that glory. We walked up to the house. On the patio, we saw a poster. "Answers to the Questions I Know You Are Asking" was the headline on the sign.

The first answer was a simple one: 50,000 bulbs, it read. The second answer was "One at a time, by one woman. Two hands, two feet, very little brain." The third answer was "Began in 1958."

There it was, The Daffodil Principle. For me, that moment was a life-changing experience. I thought of this woman whom I had never met, who, more than 40 years before, had begun–one bulb at a time –to bring her vision of beauty and joy to an obscure mountain-top. Still, just planting one bulb at a time, year after year, had changed the world. This unknown woman had forever changed the world in which she lived. She had created something indescribable: magnificence, beauty and inspiration.

The principle her daffodil garden taught is one of the greatest principles of celebration. That is, learning to move toward our goals and desires one step at a time–often just one baby-step at time–and learning to love the doing, learning to use the accumulation of time. When we multiply tiny pieces of time with small increments of daily effort, we, too, will find we can accomplish magnificent things. We can change the world.

"It makes me sad in a way," I admitted to Carolyn. "What might I have accomplished if I had thought of a wonderful goal 35 or 40 years ago and had worked away at it 'one bulb at a time' through all those years? Just think what I might have been able to achieve!"

My daughter summed up the message of the day in her usual direct way. "Start tomorrow," she said.

Like Jaroldeen, have you ever felt convicted that your life should be more productive? If so, it's pointless to think about the lost hours of "yesterdays." Rather than wallowing in regret, ask yourself, "How can I implement this today?"

The path to an exceptional life isn't a mystery. Learn to use the accumulation of time. Through small increments of daily effort, you can maximize time and accomplish magnificent things. There is a Chinese proverb that says, "A journey of a thousand miles begins with a single step."

But you must start *today.*

If we don't take hold of our limited time, our days will be devoured by random, unproductive activities. Time is disturbingly easy to waste. Novelist Robert Heinlein said, "In the absence of clearly defined goals, we become strangely loyal to performing daily trivia until we become enslaved by it." Because our time is, in fact, our very life. If we waste our time, we waste our lives.

The daffodil principle—investing regular amounts of time into important activities—can also work in reverse. Neglect is an ever-growing snowball that grows in size and velocity, bringing tremendous pain and disappointment into our lives.

The sober truth is, you can't make up for lost time. When I was in college, friends would goof off during the semester. Then at exam time, they'd pull all-nighters and cram, hoping to make up for their neglect. A few were able to pull off a decent grade, but most could not. The negative impact of negligence is far-reaching:

- A lack of discipline will get you fired, or force you to settle for less desirable jobs.
- Making small compromises, like cheating or lying, will ruin friendships and put strain on your future

marriage. Your kids will likely inherit your flaws.

- Looking at porn will (over the long haul) decrease your ability and desire to have sex in marriage. You could lose your spouse, or never get married at all.

The most important areas of your life require regular deposits of time. If you neglect these opportunities, they are lost forever. Don't let your college season slip away. These years matter. What you invest in now, little by little, will shape the rest of your life.

Questions for Reflection

1. If you were to write out a list of the top 5 things you do every day, what would make the list? Are you happy with the list, or would you change it?

2. What is something exceptional you want to accomplish in life? How can you take a step toward that goal today?

3. Is there something important in your life you've been neglecting? Since you can't make up for lost time, how can you reprioritize in order to pursue what you value?

CHAPTER 3

························

WHAT IS TRUE FREEDOM?

Freedom and the Control of Our Desires

For many students, college is all about *freedom*. They can structure their lives however they choose. No curfew! They can skip class whenever they want. No parental oversight. No annoying siblings. A chance to start fresh and be whoever they want to be.

As a college student, does freedom excite you? What *is* freedom to you?

The Oxford philosopher Isaiah Berlin identifies two types of freedom: negative and positive. Today, many people view freedom in negative terms—what they want to be free "from." Usually this means freedom from restrictions, which hold them back from fulfilling their dreams. Negative freedom says, "I'm free from everything that interferes with my desires."

On the flip side, Berlin deems *positive* freedom what we want to be free "for." Usually this means freedom to pursue what you want. For a musician, dancer or athlete, positive freedom is the ability to train, practice, and perform, whereas negative freedom would be anything that prevents those things.

Alexander the Great claimed that the Persians would always be slaves because they could never say "no." Reflecting on this, author and social critic Os Guiness writes that true freedom thrives on self-restraint and the power to say "no." A culture unable to curb its desires is a culture with no future. Guinness reveals that true freedom requires saying "no" to anything that is false, bad, excessive or destructive. Conversely, freedom is found in things that are virtuous, just, excellent, or beautiful.

We want freedom because it makes us feel like we have control—that we're the authority over our own lives. For many students, college is often a season to reject or question traditional authority figures, whether parents, teachers, government officials, or even God. Many assume that if you surrender your life to God and obey Him, He will steal your happiness. For example:

- God commands sex in marriage alone (instead of sleeping with anyone)
- God created gender as male or female (instead of seeing gender as fluid, nonbinary, or open to "self-expression")
- God asks his people to live sacrificially, not selfishly

But before dismissing God as a cosmic killjoy, ask yourself: why would the God who made us and loves us want us to be unhappy? In the Bible, Jesus tells us in John 10:10, "The thief comes only to steal and kill and destroy; I have come that they may have life, and have it to the full." Have you considered that God offers the most fulfilling life imaginable? We resist the path He lays out for us because we doubt it will actually bring us freedom. Instead, we believe God will consistently cross our wills and deprive us of our freedom. But there are times our wills *need* reshaping, for our ultimate good.

Imagine that, to get your body into better shape, you decide to exercise every day before class. Your alarm goes off the first day and you're half-awake. It feels so good to stay in bed. But you deny your desire to sleep and decide, "I am going to get out of bed, get dressed and head to the gym." It takes a lot of willpower to get up, but you do it. Later that night, as you look over the menu at a restaurant, you see several entrees that look incredible but are high in fat and calories. Because you're prioritizing your physical discipline, you say, "No! I'm going to deny my will and choose a *healthy* option." The following week, you even hire a personal trainer who helps you train more efficiently. Under his supervision, he encourages you to push through the pain, almost to the point of exhaustion, to gain greater strength.

Do you see what's happening? There are many experiences in this life that feel good in the moment but ultimately jeopardize your health. By denying your immediate desires, and making better choices, the long term benefit is immense. When you recognize this, you'll be willing to deny yourself.

This is the paradox of positive freedom. At first, self-control, boundaries, and saying "no" to yourself feel restrictive, but in the end these things deliver the best long-term results. It's wise to forfeit something of value now for the sake of something of *greater* value later. This is what Berlin means by "positive freedom."

Positive freedom can also reap rewards in your moral and spiritual life. For example, making little decisions to work hard builds strong character over time. That character will help you grow a strong business, build respect among your peers, and spare you the pain of paying hefty fees due to tax evasion. On the flipside, those who cultivate a cheating habit early on might get ahead for a while, but eventually their character catches up with them.

We were made to operate a certain way. God designed life so that it is governed by certain laws and principles, and if we live in harmony with them, our lives will flourish. For this reason, a life full of foolish and unwise choices is not freedom. As Guinness rightly observes:

> Freedom is not choice so much as right choice. When everything is permissible, no one is truly free, so it is ironic but not accidental that millions in 'the land of the free' are in recovery groups from one addiction or another.

I remember watching a great illustration a number of years ago that can help us better understand this truth. A youth director wanted to illustrate to a group of teenagers what it means to be truly free. He got a goldfish bowl that was full of water and had a single goldfish in it. He proceeded to reach into the bowl, pick up the goldfish, and drop it on the table. The fish jumped two feet into the air and then off the table onto the floor. It flipped and flopped around for a minute and then lay still as its gills were straining for oxygen. The teenagers begged him to put the fish back into the bowl.

He protested and said to the students, "But the bowl is so confining; the fish is free outside of the bowl." He finally put the fish back into the bowl and explained that only in water could the fish be free to do what a fish does. And just as a fish is made for water, we were made for God.

Here's the oft-ignored truth: Freedom to do whatever you desire actually makes you a slave. If you can't say no to something, you're a prisoner of addiction. When you are addicted to anything, you're no longer free. Addiction holds you captive and destroys your life.

Several years ago, I spoke to a large fraternity at a major university here in the South. My topic was "A Life of Excellence," and at one point in the presentation, I said, "So many young men leave college with a double addiction: alcohol and pornography." I explained that these dual addictions are a pit that will greatly hinder their marriages and careers.

When I spoke these words, there was dead silence. You could have heard a pin drop. That silence was the sound of conviction. For the first time, many of these college men realized they were slaves—slaves to the very things they thought proved they were free.

What about you? Have you discovered the power of saying "no" to lesser things, in order to say "yes" to greater things?

Questions for Reflection

1. Does the increased freedom in college excite you? How well have you managed that freedom so far?

2. As you evaluate your life, are you realizing that some of your desires have enslaved you? What is one step you can take towards freedom?

3. God alone brings true freedom into our lives—have you welcomed His work in your life, or resisted Him? How might you draw closer to Him?

3.2

....

Freedom without Restrictions

I went to college at the University of the South in Sewanee, Tennessee. It sits on top of a mountain, surrounded by magnificent, breathtaking views and serene calmness.

When I was a student, there was a local physician who owned a glider and he would get my roommate, Fred, to help him launch his plane. They would go to the local airport and Fred would pull the plane down the runway with an old station wagon. They had to reach a speed of 90 miles per hour before the doctor could release the cable and take off in the plane. At times, on a sunny day, a shadow would soundlessly flash over me while I walked on campus. Looking up, I'd see the plane, moving silently through the air. That glider was the perfect picture of freedom, as it peacefully soared over the mountain.

Why was that glider able to soar through the sky so freely? Because it was built to thrive in that environment. If you put it in water, it would sink. If you rolled it onto the freeway, it would sit motionless. Freedom is not the absence of restrictions; it's finding the *right* restrictions that allow us to soar through life as God intends.

To better understand the relationship between freedom and restrictions, consider the game of football. The game is governed by rules, and for the sake of this illustration, we'll call the rules the "Law of the Game." Imagine one day the people on the football committee are pressured to change some of the rules. People feel the current rules are too restrictive, and that the players deserve more freedom. So in response, the committee enacts three major changes.

First, they do away with facemask penalties. After all, who's to say which ones are intentional vs. unintentional? Face masks can now be grabbed at any time for any reason.

Second, they nix holding penalties, since so many holding calls are missed by referees anyway. Players are now free to hold one another whenever they want.

Finally, to enliven the return game, the committee allows players to block in the back, on kickoff and punt returns.

All of these changes are enacted in the name of freedom. But would this *really* improve the game? If you're familiar with football, you know removing these restrictions would only create more injuries. The game would devolve into chaos. Rules make football safe and enjoyable. Within the "Law of the Game," there is great freedom: You can run whatever play you want. On offense, you can be conservative or employ a hurry-up, no-huddle strategy. You can go for it on fourth down or kick it away. You can run trick plays. Defensively, you can blitz, or you can run a 3–4 or a 4–3. Ultimately, you can be as free and creative as you want—all within the "Law of the Game."

When freedom is defined as "no restrictions," people get hurt. This explains why, despite our incredible freedom today, many lives are chaotic. It explains why so many Americans are unhappy and in pain.

Emile Durkheim, one of the founders of sociology in the late nineteenth century, conducted a massive study to determine which factors affect the suicide rate. All of his findings can be summarized in one word: "constraints."

He discovered that people with fewer social constraints and obligations are *more* likely to kill themselves. To have meaning in life, people need structure. This is how God designed life to work. Freedom without restrictions is deadly, like a fish who decides to be "free" from water, or a plane that attempts to "fly" underwater.

But freedom within healthy boundaries—boundaries set up by our loving Creator—leads to a life of peace, order and harmony. Boundaries are key to finding happiness.

Questions for Reflection

1. As you go through your college journey, what important boundaries do you need to establish so you can live in freedom?

2. What are some faulty ideas about freedom on university campuses, and how can you guard yourself from embracing them?

3. Why does living for Christ offer *more* freedom than just living for yourself?

3.3

....

Freedom and the Pursuit of Happiness

M any university students believe freedom means the absence of restraints in their lives. If you just "follow your heart" and don't "hurt anyone," anything goes. In this worldview, the goal of life is to fulfill your desires at any cost.

But is this modern definition of liberty working? Author Philip Yancey, in a heartbreaking story about his older brother, writes about the dire consequences of unbridled freedom:

> In an attempt to break the shackles of a confining upbringing, he went on a grand quest for freedom, trying on worldviews like changes of clothing: Pentecostalism, atheistic existentialism, Buddhism, New Age Spirituality, Thomistic rationalism. He joined the flower children of the 1960s, growing his hair long and wearing granny glasses, living communally, experimenting with sex and drugs. For a time, he sent me exuberant reports of his new life. Eventually, however, a darker side crept in. I had to bail him out of jail when an LSD trip went bad. He broke relations with every other person in the family, and he burned through several marriages. I got late-night suicide calls. Watching my brother, I learned that

apparent freedom can actually mask deep bondage, a cry from the heart of unmet needs. The most musically gifted person I have ever known ended up tuning pianos, not playing them on a concert stage.

Yancey had a front row seat to the destructive power of unrestrained freedom. Had his brother genuinely wanted to become an accomplished musician and play in concert halls, it would have required hours and hours of practice. This would have felt restrictive in the moment, but his discipline and hard work would have unleashed his immeasurable talent to produce beautiful music.

You might never go off the rails like Yancey's brother, but ask yourself: Is my pursuit of freedom sabotaging my future? Sometimes the greatest damage isn't caused by what we're doing; it's caused by what we're NOT doing. The greatest tragedy is the sacrifice of our potential.

In the book of James (1:25), the writer speaks of the person "who looks intently into the perfect law that gives freedom." I want to highlight two words: *law and freedom*. Can a law really lead to freedom? To the modern mind, the word law sounds more confining than *liberating*. Many mistakenly believe God wants to steal our happiness, when in reality He wants to increase it.

Author Tim Keller says that, in order to gain a richer freedom, you first must give up lesser freedoms. Thus, to obey God will require you to give up some other freedoms, but in doing so, you'll discover ultimate freedom--the freedom of walking with Christ.

The human heart is complex—many of our desires stand in opposition to each other. For example, as a girl you might want to marry the man of your dreams one day, but you might also want to date every good-looking guy you meet. Competing interests require that you choose a side. As we weigh the competing desires of our hearts, it's critical for us to discern which desires are liberating and which are destructive. Are we chasing desires that shape us into who we want to be, or someone else?

Questions for Reflection

1. Why do you think the words "law" and "freedom" are viewed as opposites? As this chapter explains, how might law actually *create* freedom?

2. People often embrace a choice "as long as it doesn't hurt anyone." Naturally, the desire to avoid harming another person is noble, but where does this cultural mantra fall short? Where is it naive?

3. Do you believe that Christ offers ultimate happiness? Where do you doubt this? How have you experienced this truth?

CHAPTER 4

PRINCIPLES TO FOLLOW

4.1

·········

Social Intelligence

I f there was one thing that could make your college experience successful, what would it be? It's a good question.
If you ask college counselors, you'll get a multitude of answers like academic focus, a vibrant social life, clear goals,
choosing the right major. All these factors are important,
but recently I stumbled upon an insight that intrigued me.

The observation came from an article in *The Wall Street
Journal* exploring the reasons people fail. Interestingly, one
of the top reasons given was a person's *inability to relate to
others.* Authors Carole Hyatt and Linda Gottlieb make this
same point in their book, *When Smart People Fail:*

> Most careers involve other people. You can have great
> academic intelligence and still lack social intelligence—
> the ability to be a good listener, to be sensitive toward
> others, to give and take criticism well.
>
> If people don't like you, they may help you fail...
> On the other hand, you can get away with serious
> mistakes if you are socially intelligent...A mistake
> may actually further [your] career if the boss thinks
> [you] handled the situation in a mature and responsi-
> ble way.

The phrase "social intelligence" is insightful. It's a form of wisdom. It's a skill that enables you to be effective in relating to and interacting with other people. If you have social intelligence, people will be drawn to you and desire your friendship.

For example, you have an unreasonable roommate who is very messy and inconsiderate, yet incessantly complains about your habits. You've tried to reason with them but they won't listen. Social intelligence says: Stop trying to win a losing battle. Kindly listen to their concerns, knowing that nothing you can say will make a difference, then move on with your day. Social intelligence recognizes where your roommate is at, takes it into account, and doesn't waste relational bandwidth.

The big question is, are you socially intelligent? Do you interact well with people? When you meet someone for the first time do you take a genuine interest in them? Do you ask insightful questions? Are you a good listener? I find that those who are not socially intelligent are generally not aware of it.

Anglican bishop J.C. Ryle says:

A person's heart is never in such a hopeless condition as when they are totally unaware of their flaws.

Research from the Carnegie Foundation for the Advancement of Teaching reveals that social intelligence can actually advance your career. In a person's profession, 15% of their financial success is due to technical knowledge and the other 85% is due to skills in human interaction and leadership ability.

Dale Carnegie's *How To Win Friends And Influence People*, arguably the most popular book ever written on human interaction, highlights the benefits of social intelligence:

> For many years, I conducted courses each season at the Engineers' Club of Philadelphia, and also courses for the New York Chapter of the American Institute of Electrical Engineers. A total of probably more than fifteen hundred engineers have passed through my classes. They came to me because they had finally realized, after years of observation and experience, that the highest-paid personnel in engineering are frequently not those who know the most about engineering. One can for example, hire mere technical ability in engineering, accountancy, architecture or any other profession at nominal salaries. But the person who has technical knowledge plus the ability to express ideas, to assume leadership, and to arouse enthusiasm among people—that person is headed for higher earning power.

John D. Rockefeller is widely considered the wealthiest American of all time. He founded the Standard Oil Company in 1870, which later became Exxon. Rockefeller viewed excellent people skills as indispensable: "The ability to deal with people is as purchasable as a commodity of sugar or coffee. And I will pay more for that ability than for any other under the sun."

Think about how you interact with people and how well you get along with them. Are you a good listener, or do you talk too much? Do you encourage others? Do you take an interest in their lives? Are you humble, or always seeking to exalt yourself? Are you reliable, doing what you say you will? Are you a team player? Do you tell others how much you appreciate their friendship?

I think author John Maxwell says it best:

> If you haven't learned how to get along with people, you will always be fighting a battle to succeed. However, making people skills a strength will take you farther than any other skill you develop. People like to do business with people they like. Or to put it the way President Theodore Roosevelt did: 'The most important single ingredient in the formula of success is knowing how to get along with people.'

Those who increase their social intelligence in college will benefit from it for the rest of their lives. Relationships matter.

Questions for Reflection

1. How would you rate your own social intelligence? Who is someone who can provide you with honest feedback about yourself?

2. How is social intelligence different from just trying to make people like you?

3. How have you seen strong relationships open up opportunities in your life? How can you continue to cultivate meaningful relationships with coworkers and friends?

4.2

....

A Prescription for Misery

Have you heard of a man named Charlie Munger? He's a 97-year-old billionaire who is the vice chairman of Berkshire Hathaway, one of the world's most successful holding companies. Warren Buffet, chairman and CEO of Berkshire Hathaway, considers Munger to be one of the wisest, most knowledgeable people he's ever known.

In 1986, Munger gave a commencement address at Harvard that was quite humorous and full of sound wisdom. His theme was "Prescription for Misery." He explained that the surest path to a miserable life is to be *unreliable.* Unreliability is the best way to sabotage your life and your relationships.

Munger said if you master this one habit—being unreliable—it will override all your other virtues, however great they may be. He said it's the best way to be distrusted and excluded. He said if you can become expertly unreliable, even mediocre people will outperform you.

To master this habit, never be on time. Don't meet deadlines. Fail to honor your commitments. Above all, don't do what you say you will.

On the flipside, Munger said it's hard to be miserable if you're responsible, even if you have certain disadvantages in your life. His college roommate was severely dyslexic, and even though he had to navigate a learning disability, Munger said, "He is perhaps the most reliable person I have ever known. He has a wonderful life so far: outstanding wife and children, [and he's the] chief executive of a multibillion-dollar corporation."

A great example of Munger's call to reliability hit the news two years ago. It took place in the suburbs of Birmingham, Alabama, where I live.

Twenty-year-old Walter Carr, who attended Lawson State started having car trouble. The next day was supposed to be the first day of his new job with Bellhops Movers. He was scheduled to be at work at 8:00 a.m. to help move a family to their new home. He called some friends to see if he could find a ride, but no one was available. It was getting close to midnight, and it looked like he wouldn't make it to the job site the next morning.

However, this new job was important to him. He didn't want to let down his new employer. He had assured them he would be there at 8:00 a.m. sharp, and he intended to keep that promise. He checked Google Maps to see how long it would take him to walk: 7 hours. He left his home at midnight and started walking to his job site over 20 miles away.

As he followed U.S. Highway 280, he was questioned by several police officers who wanted to know why he was walking alone in the middle of the night. After hearing his story, one policeman took him first to breakfast, then drove Walter the rest of the way to the home of Jenny and Chris Lamey, who were packing up to move to a new home. Jenny Lamey was impressed with Carr and his story, and they quickly developed a bond. In an article in the *Pelham Reporter*, Lamey said:

I just can't tell you how touched I was by Walter and his journey. He is humble and kind and cheerful, and he has big dreams! He is hardworking and tough. I can't imagine how many times on that lonely walk down 280 in the middle of the night did he want to turn back. How many times did he wonder if this was the best idea? How many times did he want to find a place to sit or lie down and wait till morning when he could maybe get someone to come pick him up and bring him back home. But he walked until he got here! I am in total awe of this young man!

The next day she posted about the experience on Facebook. Luke Marklin, CEO of Bellhops Movers, was so blown away by Carr's efforts, he drove his own Ford Escort down from Tennessee to personally give it to Walter. Carr wasn't prepared for the outpouring of support and media attention and was moved to tears.

Since then, he's been featured on CNN, Fox News, NBC's Today Show, the BBC and more. He's received multiple job offers and scholarships. Before he even had a Twitter account, he was the subject of tweets from Alabama Governor Kay Ivey, as well as US Ambassador to the UN, Nikki Haley.

Jenny Lamey even set up a GoFundMe for Walter. Out of a desire to bless others, Walter pledged that when the account reached over $65,000, any additional monies received would go to the Birmingham Ed Foundation (a nonprofit dedicated to increasing the number of students in Birmingham City Schools that are on the path to college, career, and life readiness). The GoFundMe account raised close to $92,000.

Walter Carr embodies Charlie Munger's advice about being reliable. He just wanted to show up on time and honor the commitment he made. He was humble, yet his story has now touched the hearts of thousands. He never set out to make a lot of money, but his reliability resulted in a financial windfall. So, if you want to succeed in life, be like Walter. Be reliable.

Questions for Reflection

1. If someone polled twenty of your closest friends, co-workers, and family members, would they describe you as reliable or unreliable? Why?

2. If reliability usually leads to a better life, why are so many people unreliable?

3. What is one thing you can do this week to become more reliable?

4.3

....

The Progress Paradox

A number of years ago, *Forbes Magazine* celebrated 75 years as a publication. You'd expect a celebratory issue to reminisce about the biggest business feats of the previous decades. Ironically, they titled this special edition "Why We Feel So Bad When We Have It So Good." The entire publication was a series of essays by philosophers, journalists, and social scientists. They analyzed why Americans don't feel good about themselves and their lives, even though they lived in unprecedented prosperity.

Since World War II, the prosperity of our nation has soared. Despite this fact, the mental, emotional, psychological, and spiritual condition of our people has plummeted, and social scientists struggle to explain why this is the case. It seems logical that mental health would coincide with material wealth, but it isn't always true. Why?

In his book, *Margin*, Dr. Richard Swenson says that in our enthusiasm about modern progress, we often overlook its negative effect on human relationships. We tend to think of progress in terms of economics, education and technology. But little thought is given to how progress impacts our relationships with others or our relationship with God. As Swenson puts it, "None of the tools of progress has helped build the relational foundation our society requires."

I'm amazed by the technology that now allows me to deposit a check into the bank from my smartphone. I can literally do this from anywhere, anytime. But think about it. Before this technology existed, I developed a pleasant relationship with the branch manager and tellers at my bank. Because of this progress, I might never interact with them again.

Cultural commentators are always eager to point out the benefits of modern progress. But in our relentless pursuit of the bottom line, we've neglected the importance of relational health. While progress has marched forward, relationships have drifted apart.

In *Margin*, Swenson makes another great observation. He says most of our progress is made in two areas:

> The first is the *physical environment*, which includes wealth, technology, and health (the material world). The second is the *cognitive environment*, which includes knowledge, information, and education (the intellectual world). I would add to this the *entertainment environment*, which includes the myriad of digital delights that constantly vie for our attention.

Most modern progress happens in those two areas (physical and cognitive), yet Swenson points out that we experience all of our *pain* in three other environments, where progress offers little help.

The first is the *social environment*, made up of family, friends, and neighbors (the societal world). Second, there's the *emotional environment*, composed of feelings and attitudes (the psychological world). Lastly, there's the *spiritual environment*, made up of the eternal and transcendent (the spiritual world).

Clearly, progress is being made in the material and cognitive environment, but the pain we suffer is found within the social, emotional, and spiritual environments. Swenson concludes:

> The material and cognitive environments are unquestionably important. They also have an advantage in that they are more visible and thus more highly pursued. The Bible teaches us, however, that the social, emotional, and spiritual environments are more important. A crucial task for our society today is to reverse the order of emphasis and visibility of these environments.

The problem is, not many people are calling for this reversal of priorities. Until we do, we will continue to be perplexed over the fact that outwardly, life seems to be getting better, but inwardly, people continue to feel worse and worse.

Questions for Reflection

1. Do you agree that putting progress first often impacts relationships negatively? Why or why not?

2. As a college student, what might it look like to pursue spiritual and relational health more than material wealth?

3. How does God want us to approach progress? What does the Bible teach about it?

4.4

....

Decisions and Choices

At 18 years old, Jane Lucretia D'Esterre, talented and beautiful, was just entering the prime of her life. One day she stood on the bank of a glistening, dark lake in Scotland, contemplating whether she should plunge in and end her life. The year was 1815. Jane's husband John had just been killed in a duel, leaving her penniless and alone in a new country with two babies to care for. Her family lived in France, so she was without support of any kind. She had lost all hope.

As she gazed into the rippling waters of the lake, reflecting on her crumbling life, she looked up and spotted a young man on the other side of the lake plowing furrows on a hillside. He was completely focused on his work, unaware he had an audience as he diligently guided the plow behind the horse.

In her moment of despair, the unknowing plowboy became a salvific metaphor for her life. She knew what she needed to do: move straight ahead like the young plowman, because she too had a meaningful task to fulfill. Her children needed her. Having already lost their father, they didn't need to experience the agony of losing a mother too. The young man's focus gave her courage to do the right thing, even though it was difficult.

A few weeks after this experience at the lake, Jane came to faith in Christ. She eventually remarried, becoming the wife of Captain John Grattan Guinness, the youngest son of the famous brewer Arthur Guinness. Prominent author Os Guinness, Jane's great-great-grandson, made this observation:

> If it had not been for the plowman, the tragedy of the dueling husband would have been followed by the tragedy of the duelist's widow...My great-great-grandmother was unusual for several reasons including the fact that she conscientiously prayed for her descendants down through a dozen generations. Ours is a heritage of faith, which I, for one, am extremely grateful.

When Jane was a heartbroken teenager contemplating suicide, her future looked as empty and dark as the waters of the lake before her. She felt her life was finished, but it wasn't. After seeing the determined young plowman, she caught a glimpse of hope.

Jane had no idea what the future held, nor could she imagine having another husband who would deeply love her and her children. She could only see the two choices before her: death in the lake or life outside it. Her decision would not only impact her life, but also the lives of her children and the generations to follow.

We rarely ponder the significance of our choices. Yet they always have consequences. Our decisions determine the ultimate outcome of our lives and, in some cases, the lives of many others. The prophet Isaiah says that we will all "eat the fruit of our actions" (Isaiah 3:10). King David compares poor decisions to falling into a deep hole we've dug ourselves (Psalm 7:15).

One of the most dangerous pitfalls we fall into is rejecting God's authority and trying to run our lives apart from him. C.S. Lewis describes how a person falls into this hole: "He has tried to set up on his own, to behave as if he belonged to himself." It's like the way pop star Miley Cyrus approaches life in her song *We Can't Stop:*

> *It's our party, we can do what we want to*
> *It's our house, we can love who we want to*
> *It's our song, we can sing if we want to*
> *It's my mouth, I can say what I want to*

When we ignore God and His will for our lives, it's like digging ourselves into an inescapable ditch. Many people believe that if you defy God, He is going to bury you. However, in reality you end up burying yourself. Much of the pain and sorrow we experience is the result of our own misguided choices.

Psychologist Chris Thurman points out how celebrities, whose lives many covet, often tend to wreck their lives through poor decisions:

> Have you ever noticed how prominent sport stars', businessmen's, politicians', and even ministers' lives implode because of scandal and moral failure? In retrospect, in almost every case, we can clearly see the seeds of their downfall sown along the way.

He says it happens slowly—an innocuous action here, a careless behavior there. Thurman adds: "...small seeds of moral carelessness sown along life's path that eventually grow into weeds of destruction." The Christian rock band, Casting Crowns, express this same idea in their song, *Slow Fade:*

74

It's a slow fade
When you give yourself away
It's a slow fade
When black and white have turned to grey
And thoughts invade, choices made
A price will be paid
When you give yourself away
People never crumble in a day
It's a slow fade

Take a moment and think about your life. Is there any area where your values or integrity are slowly eroding? Most people don't realize that the corruption of our soul happens slowly and subtly over time.

If you discover an area of your life where things are headed in the wrong direction, are you willing to change your behavior and mentality in that area? It's one thing to notice destructive patterns in yourself; it's another thing entirely to do something about it. Start making changes today.

Every choice you make has consequences that will come back to you. Make sure they are good consequences that build the life you ultimately want to have. And rest assured that in all circumstances, good or bad, God will be faithful to you.

Questions for Reflection

1. Are there habits of compromise in your life that you've been ignoring? What is God calling you to do about it?

2. Is the idea of God's authority over your life encouraging or threatening? Why? _____

3. What would it look like to submit your decisions to God's authority—to trust Him with *all* of your life?

4.5

....

Be a Student for Life

What does it take to get a job at Google? That's exactly what Thomas Friedman set out to discover in his *New York Times* article "How to Get a Job at Google." He interviewed Laszlo Bock, Google's former Senior Vice President of hiring, to get a rare inside perspective on the company's hiring strategy.

During the conversation Bock shared insights about what actually sets candidates apart: "GPAs are worthless as a criterion for hiring and test scores are worthless; we found they don't predict anything."

So what *does* it take to get a job at Google? According to Bock, *humility*. They want courageous leaders who will step up and lead, but who are also willing to relinquish power when appropriate. In other words, they need to be humble enough to admit when the ideas of others are better than their own.

This idea, of acknowledging your own limitations, as well as the strengths of others, is called *intellectual humility*. If you don't have intellectual humility, you won't be able to learn when you fail. Too many proud people take credit when something good happens, but blame others when something bad happens.

Someone with intellectual humility realizes there's a lot they don't know. They're always seeking to learn and grow. They're on a relentless quest for improvement. On the other hand, intellectually arrogant people over-esteem themselves. They listen poorly and learn slowly. They believe their current knowledge and ability are sufficient, assuming there isn't much more they need to learn. This applies to college life; intellectual arrogance often dominates classrooms. The irony is, in a place where everyone is supposed to be a learner, people act like they know it all.

Charlie Munger, who I referenced in a previous chapter, delivered another commencement speech to law school students at the University of Southern California in 2007. In it he tells the students, "It is crucial to be hooked on lifetime learning." As an example of this principle, he mentions Warren Buffet, the CEO of Berkshire Hathaway, which he calls "the best regarded company in the world, with the best investment record in the history of civilization." Munger says that Buffett spends half of his waking time reading and a big chunk of the rest of his time talking to knowledgeable people all over the world. In other words, Warren Buffet is "a continuous learning machine."

Munger believes this attribute can be developed and applied by any person. He says:

I constantly see people rise in life who are not the smartest, sometimes not even the most diligent. But they are learning machines. They go to bed every night a little wiser than they were that morning. And boy, does that habit help, particularly when you have a long run ahead of you.

Nine-time Grammy and Pulitzer Prize-winning jazz musician Wynton Marsalis offers this advice to aspiring musicians who want to become great:

> Humility engenders learning because it beats back the arrogance that puts blinders on. It leaves you open for truths to reveal themselves. You don't stand in your own way ... Do you know how you can tell if someone is truly humble? I believe there's one simple test: because they consistently observe and listen, the humble improve. They don't assume, 'I know the way.'

Humble people are students for life. They seek to learn from everyone and everything. It might be from people who excel in your field or even from those less successful than you. Wherever you are in your life journey, if you adopt the perspective of intellectual humility, every moment of every day will be a chance to grow, improve, and learn.

Questions for Reflection

1. Do you think you have intellectual humility? When was the last time you relinquished your ideas to embrace the ideas of someone else?

2. Do you know anyone who is successful and humble? What qualities and habits do you see at work in their life?

3. What is one practical way you can pursue humility at your college, with your roommate, in a relationship, or at your job?

CHAPTER 5

HUMAN SEXUALITY

5.1

·········

Are There Any Rules for Sex?

Sex is awesome! Most college students would agree with that statement, but few would expect God to agree with that statement. Yet scripture is clear that God is the Author of sex, which is meant to be expressed within the covenant of marriage.

God isn't the only one who thinks sex works best with some boundaries in place. Jordan Peterson, an author and psychologist whose lectures and interviews have gone viral in the last few years, shares in an interview why promiscuous, unhindered sex is dangerous:

> We've had relatively reliable birth control since 1960. That's not very long, and we underestimate the unbelievable technological triumph of birth control. It's the hydrogen bomb: it's the transistor: it's a major-league transformation in human interaction. Women are now free from involuntary reproduction. That's never been the case in the entire history of the planet.
>
> We don't know exactly what to do about that. So, the first idea in the 60's was, let's party, and you know, you could see why. It's like, the rules for not engaging in promiscuous sexual intercourse seemed to have

vanished, so we had a couple of decades of experimentation. Well, how'd that go?

A little hard on the family I would say. That's not so good for kids. AIDS. That wasn't a plus; it could have killed us all. And it mutated, particularly to take advantage of promiscuous sex, because viruses are very tricky things. So, it turns out that sex is a little bit more complicated than we thought. Well, it actually turns out that it's a lot more complicated than we thought.

Now it's 40, 50, 60 years later, and we're trying to sort this out. It's like, well, when is it okay to have sex? And when is it not okay to have sex, and what does it mean that it's okay, and what does consent mean, and the answer to that is, well, we never used to have to think these things through because the rule was don't have sex until you get married. That was the rule. Now, that isn't the rule? So, what's the rule? Well, we're not having a conversation about the rule.

Peterson's words remind me of American author George Leonard, who was a big proponent of the sexual liberation movement. He believed in complete sexual freedom—that people should enjoy sex with multiple partners. He would have been an enthusiastic advocate of the hookup culture we live in today.

But years later, Leonard wrote a book titled *The End of Sex: Erotic Love after the Sexual Revolution*. Leonard says:

I have finally come to see that every game has a rule, and sex has rules. Unless you play by the rules, you'll find sex can create a depth of loneliness that nothing else can.

Think of all the damage done by the misuse of our sexuality: sexually transmitted disease, teen pregnancy, abortion, psychological damage from rape, sexual abuse, incest, sexual addictions, and pornography. Many have known the bitter betrayal of a spouse who cheated on them. Likewise, many children watch their families splinter after one of their parents commits adultery.

I am reminded of pastor Ray Ortlund's words:

"Sex is like fire. In the fireplace it keeps us warm. Outside the fireplace it burns down the house."

But all this pain and guilt can be avoided by following God's guidelines for sex. Many people today live without any standards for sexual conduct. This is why I find both Peterson's and Leonard's words about rules for sex to be so intriguing. If sex has rules, and ignoring these rules leads to painful consequences, then one must ask two simple questions: What are the rules, and who makes them?

Many people today don't realize that sex was God's idea. But if sex was His idea, then He must have a plan that leads to the healthiest and greatest sexual experience.

Several Hebrew words (the language the Old Testament is written in), help express God's vision for sex in marriage. For example, when the Bible mentions that a husband has sex with his wife, the English translation generally is, "He lays with her." But the actual Hebrew word for sex in the text is *yada*, meaning "to know, to be known, to be deeply respected." Thus, from the Bible's perspective sex isn't *only* about physical pleasure; it's also about relational intimacy.

Another frequently-used Hebrew word is *hesed*, which means "deep friendship and loyalty." In scripture, God often describes His relationship with His people as a marriage, and *hesed* is the word used to encapsulate His love. Though God's relationship with us is covenantal, not sexual, He designed sex for us to enjoy. Sex between married partners is an expression of intimate love between best friends.

In Matthew 19:4-5, Jesus quotes Genesis 2:24, which says: "He who created them from the beginning made them male and female, and said for this reason a man shall leave his father and mother and cleave to his wife, and the two shall become one flesh."

This passage includes a third, helpful Hebrew word. The word cleave is translated from the Hebrew word *dabaq*, meaning "absolute unity." To cleave to someone is to say, "I completely belong to you. Exclusively! Permanently! Everything I have is yours. I am yours." It's total connection and solidarity.

Everyone longs for this level of intimacy, and God's plan provides the best way for us to experience it, as author Philip Yancey explains:

> Our desires, including sexual desires, are not wrong. They are, rather, like the rungs of a ladder that lead us toward beauty, toward relationship and intimacy, and ultimately toward God who granted us these gifts. Remove the rungs from the ladder, though, and you are left with scattered sticks of wood leading nowhere.

By God's good design, sex enables us to truly cleave to another person. And because that level of permanent intimacy should be shared only with the person you've committed to for life, God's plan is for sex to be reserved for marriage. For those willing to heed His plan, sex is a wonderful gift.

Questions for Reflection

1. Since God created sex, and intended it to be enjoyed in the context of marriage, what does that say about His character? What does it say about His goodness?

   _____

   _____

2. Why are rules (or boundaries) concerning sex a helpful thing? What harm comes when rules for sex are ignored?

   _____

   _____

3. What actions or beliefs is God calling you to when it comes to sex?

   _____

   _____

Sex and the Pursuit
of Happiness

O ur views on sex and human sexuality have changed
dramatically over the last 60 years. In the 1950's, there
was a an accepted moral standard when it came to sexual behavior. Sex within marriage was the expected norm.
Though people had sex outside of marriage and adultery
was commonplace, it was still widely considered to be
morally wrong.

All of that has changed. Today, for single people (and
even for some who are married), sex has devolved from
a sacred act to just another form of recreation. For many,
sex exists for the sole purpose of providing pleasure. God
created sex to be wonderfully pleasurable, which is a gift,
but society has stripped it of its beauty and purpose. People desire to be sexually free—to hook up with no strings
attached.

Sigmund Freud believed that the purpose of life is to
be happy, and that genital sex is the primary source of all
human happiness. Many think Freud's teachings catalyzed
the sexual revolution of the 1960's. That revolution has
vastly influenced today's view of sex and created a culture
that believes that sexual pleasure (whether experienced in
person or through pornography) is essential to our well-being and happiness.

Ironically, most people don't realize that Freud's views on sex eventually shifted. Later in life he remarked that, when sexual standards disappear, we experience the same thing that happened "in the decline of ancient civilization, [when] love became worthless and life empty."

Surprisingly, Freud actually raised his children with clear-cut sexual boundaries. According to Dr. Armand Nicholi, who studied his life in great detail, ultimately Freud concluded that restraint, not indulgence, leads to happiness.

At this stage in my life, I conclude that pleasure can bring temporary delight into your life, but not lasting happiness. The demand for pleasure is forever at war with reality. It has the potential to enslave you and over time, destroy you.

To fully understand how the cultural consensus about sex has transformed, we must go back nearly 2,700 years to a single sentence spoken by the Old Testament prophet Isaiah. His words could have been written for us today:

Woe to those who call evil good, and good, evil; who substitute darkness for light, and light for darkness; who substitute bitter for sweet, and sweet for bitter! (Isaiah 5:20)

Author David Wells echoes Isaiah's thoughts, defining worldliness as "that which makes righteousness look strange and sin look normal." This is precisely what the media, Hollywood and those who create our entertainment have done. They have taken what God has said is healthy, beautiful, and good, and they have made it appear antiquated, boring, and narrow-minded. God gives us commands and sets boundaries for a reason, but the secular world minimizes the consequences of sex and overstates its benefits. The world has taken what God has said is wrong, evil and unhealthy and has made it appear to be exciting and fulfilling.

When was the last time you saw a movie or television program depicting a married couple with a vibrant sex life? Hollywood tends to highlight dysfunctional relationships, infidelity, or sex that has no boundaries. As a result, people believe this somehow makes for a thrilling life.

Likewise, the church has often blushed about sex, rather than promoting it as a joyful gift within marriage. Its silence on sexual pleasure has allowed Hollywood to disciple people, rather than God's Word.

Consider how college students react when they hear the phrase "sexual purity." Typically they respond with disdain and sarcasm: what a prudish concept! But we should be wary of stereotyping purity. Author and missionary Elisabeth Elliot shares some profound words about the surprising meaning of this word in the context of human sexuality:

Purity means freedom from contamination, from anything that would spoil the taste of pleasure, reduce the power, or in any way cheapen what the thing was meant to be. It means cleanness; clearness; no additives; nothing artificial; in other words, all natural; in the sense in which the Designer designed it to be.

In reading this, several things catch my attention: the word "contamination" and the phrase "reduce the power."

When you think of the future with your spouse—your soul mate—do you want to risk contaminating and reducing the power of your future sex life? That's what's at stake. Reading Elliot's message for the first time, I thought, "This is really what I want for my children." Then, it struck me. This is also what I want for my own marriage. This is what God offers when we live our lives according to His design.

No doubt college will present countless opportunities to experiment sexually, but I encourage you to trust God. He wants your happiness more than anyone, including yourself. Follow His plan for sex, and you'll never regret it.

Questions for Reflection

1. David Wells defines worldliness as "anything that makes righteousness look strange and sin look normal." Have you fallen into this trap when it comes to sex, and how might God desire to reshape your thinking?

2. How is God's ideal for sex (reserved for two married people) more satisfying than modern hookup culture?

3. Although sexual purity is often stereotyped as a prudish concept, why is it something worth pursuing? How will you pursue sexual purity in your life, especially during college?

5.3

....

The Beauty of Discovery

Hookup culture has changed our view of sex. This is particularly true on college campuses. But how is hookup culture working out for college students? Even feminist Naomi Wolf believes the new sexuality is having a devastating impact on young adults. She says, "We have raised a generation of young women and men, who don't understand sexual ethics. They don't see sex as sacred or even important anymore. Sex has been commodified and drained of its deeper meaning."

In this essay, I want to share some new insights that I believe will provide some wisdom when it comes to sexuality. The first comes from Ecclesiastes 7:8, which was written by King Solomon: "One man among a thousand I have found, but a woman among all these I have not found." Reflecting on this verse, Bible scholar Ray Stedman makes the following comment:

> We must read this carefully. As he [Solomon] went through life he occasionally found a loyal, trustworthy, godly, wise man who could be a true friend, a man of integrity, but he never found a woman like that; out of the thousand women he was involved with, he never found one whom he could trust. Why?

Solomon's problem wasn't caused by a lack of trustworthy women in his kingdom—his problem came from the fact that he had 700 wives and 300 concubines (1 Kings 11:3). Instead of relating wholeheartedly with one wife Solomon's excessive sexual appetite prevented him from truly connecting with any woman. It's impossible to imagine that, while sleeping with 1,000 women, Solomon had the ability to build deep relationships with any of his wives.

Because Solomon rotated sexual partners so frequently, he never discovered what Stedman calls "continuous discovery," which refers to the ever-deepening friendship of two lovers who commit to one another for a lifetime. To have sex prematurely "arrests the mutual process of discovery." You cannot learn who the other person really is if you have sexual relations before the proper time. The same is true if, like Solomon, you're constantly seeking new sexual exploits—one eye constantly on the horizon.

The beauty of discovery leads to depth and intimacy in our relationships. Within marriage, a healthy sexual relationship enhances the discovery process. Outside of the commitment and intimacy of marriage, sex ends up derailing discovery.

Our society in general doesn't take this into consideration. They do not seek to follow God's wisdom when it comes to sex. We all want to experience the richness of life, yet so many of us seek it outside of the boundaries God put in place. We simply cannot enjoy the fullness of what God intended for our lives if we live out of alignment with His plan.

We cannot experience the beauty of discovery, which leads to depth and intimacy in our relationships, unless we pursue each other as God designed. Everyone wants to experience total security in a romantic relationship—to know they're completely loved, accepted, and protected. Hookup culture makes this impossible.

I once heard pastor Charles Swindoll share about an actor who was well-known for his romantic roles on film. In a talk show interview, the actor was predictably asked, "What makes a great lover?" Swindoll (and everyone else watching) expected a playboy response. Surprisingly, his answer shattered the promiscuous paradigm expected from a Hollywood icon:

> A great lover is someone who can satisfy one woman all her life long and who can be satisfied by one woman all his life long. A great lover is not someone who goes from woman to woman to woman. Any dog can do that.

No one was prepared for that answer. To some, it sounded far-fetched and confining, but actually, research reveals the societal benefits of lifelong monogamy.

In 1934, prominent scholar J.D. Unwin had spent many years studying eighty-six civilizations. He published his findings in a book called *Sex and Culture*, which documented a direct tie between "absolute heterosexual monogamy" and the "expansive energy" of civilization. In every culture he studied, sexual fidelity was the single most important predictor of a society's dominion and strength. Unwin had no religious bias or agenda. "I offer no opinion about rightness or wrongness," he said. Nevertheless, he concluded: "In human records there is no instance of a society retaining its energy after a complete new generation has inherited a tradition which does not insist on prenuptial and postnuptial sexual restraint."

Clearly, civilizations flourish when they prioritize fidelity in marriage. And considering our culture's celebration of same-sex marriage, Unwin's reference to "absolute heterosexual monogamy" is very specific to mean marriage between one man and one woman. Unwin had hundreds of years of history to draw upon, including Roman, Greek, Sumerian, Moorish, Babylonian, and Anglo-Saxon civilizations. *He found no exceptions.* These societies flourished, culturally and geographically, during eras that valued sexual fidelity. Inevitably, as sexual standards loosened, societies subsequently crumbled. If they rose back to prominence, it was typically linked to a resurgence of sexual morality.

> Unwin had difficulty explaining the pattern. "If you ask me why this is so, I reply that I do not know. No scientist does. You can describe the process and observe it, but you cannot explain it." After reading Unwin's book, Philip Yancey commented:

Unwin preached a message that few people want to hear. Without realizing it, though, Unwin may have subtly edged toward a Christian view of sexuality from which modern society has badly strayed. For the Christian, sex is not an end in itself, but rather a gift of God. Like such gifts, it must be stewarded according to God's rules, not ours.

Christianity teaches that there is a divinely established moral order and that we, as human beings, can't define morality on our own. When we choose to defy God's moral order, we pay a great price. Though hookup culture promises to satisfy, history proves the opposite. If you will honor God's vision for sex, you will find true satisfaction.

Questions for Reflection

1. What sexual sin do you need to confess to God right now? Do so, knowing that His forgiveness is complete. (1 John 1:9)

   ....

   ....

2. Why is God's vision for monogamy (marriage to one person) better than the world's vision of promiscuity?

   ....

   ....

3. Who in your life can encourage you to embrace a life of purity? How can you reach out and connect with that person or group?

   ....

   ....

5.4

How to Ruin Your Sex Life

Pornography can wreck your life. For some, the devastating effects of their porn addiction isn't understood until marriage. I once heard a couple speak about how pornography almost ruined their marriage. Their struggles led to divorce, but after walking through a healing process, their marriage was restored six years later. They now lead a ministry for families and individuals caught in the jaws of porn addiction. Pornography is a silent but destructive force in the lives of many people. I describe it as silent because it is usually kept secret until things begin to fall apart.

Porn affects all ages—even the young. I spoke to a man who was working with a group of sixth-grade boys in his church. He had them anonymously fill out a survey. One of the questions was, "Have you watched pornography in the past?" All of them answered "yes." He informed their parents (most of whom had no idea), so they could follow up with their children.

My heart breaks to recall the couple who were both virgins on their wedding day, but on the first night of their honeymoon, the husband couldn't perform sexually. He reluctantly shared that he had been addicted to pornography for years. Can you imagine being confronted with such a devastating marital obstacle on your very first day as husband and wife?

Supermodel Christie Brinkley, considered by many to be one of the most physically attractive women in the world and featured three times on the cover of *Sports Illustrated Swimsuit Edition,* married architect Peter Cook. Peter had a $3,000-a-month porn habit, which likely paved the way for his eventual affair with a teenager. Cook was married to one of the most beautiful women in the world but still looked to porn to satisfy his sexual desires, ultimately destroying his marriage.

An experienced, well-regarded counselor recently told me that pornography is the 500-pound gorilla in the world of addiction. He said that pornography addiction is easy to hide from others, is very difficult to overcome, and can have devastating effects on your relationships. Both men and women are graduating from college heavily addicted to pornography. Since internet porn is still relatively new, we're just beginning to understand how pornography impacts regular users, particularly those who have viewed it for years.

Some argue that pornography has no effect on individuals who consume it, but they're essentially saying people are not influenced by what they see, and we know that isn't true. The advertising industry spends billions every year to put things in front of your eyes, knowing that what we see impacts what we desire.

In their book, *The Porn Trap,* sex therapists Wendy and Larry Maltz share that people are shocked when they first hear about the destructive force of pornography. Many consider it harmless fun; it's not a drug, alcoholic drink, or even an authentic sexual experience. So how destructive can it be? The Maltzes explain how, even though pornography looks benign, it actually changes your brain chemistry. It rewires the way you think. It stimulates the hedonic highway, the area of the brain where the chemical dopamine is released during sexual arousal. Pornography causes a huge spike of dopamine production in the brain that's comparable to the high one gets from using cocaine. The Maltzes further add:

> Porn's power to produce experiences of excitement, relaxation and escape from pain make it highly addictive. Over time you can come to depend on it to feel good and require it so you don't feel bad. Cravings, preoccupations and out-of-control behavior with using it can become commonplace. Porn sex can become your greatest need. If you have been using porn regularly to "get high," withdrawal from porn can be as filled with agitation, depression and sleeplessness as detoxing from alcohol, cocaine and other hard drugs. In fact, people in porn recovery take an average of 18 months to heal from the damage to their dopamine receptors alone.

Ironically, one of the most documented consequences of porn is it's negative impact on sexual desire and function. Naomi Wolf's *New York* magazine article, "The Porn Myth," says this:

> You would think porn would make men into raving beasts. On the contrary, the onslaught of porn is responsible for deadening male libido in relation to real women and leading men to see fewer and fewer women as porn-worthy. Women are not having to fend

off porn-crazed men but are having a hard time keeping their attention.

Dr. Ursula Ofman, a Manhattan-based sex therapist, shares about the devastating effects porn is having on her male patients:

> It's so accessible, and now, with things like streaming video and webcams, guys are getting sucked into a compulsive behavior. What's most regrettable is that it can really affect relationships with women. I've seen some young men lately who can't get aroused with women but have no problem interacting with the Internet.

In her well-researched book, *Pornified*, journalist Pamela Paul says:

> While some men try to keep pornography and real sex separate in their heads, it's not so easy; pornography seeps in, sometimes in unexpected ways. The incursion can even lead to sexual problems, such as impotence or delayed ejaculation.

Sex therapist and psychologist Aline Zoldbrod is convinced that a vast number of young men are destined to be terrible lovers because of pornography. Too many men assume women will respond to them as the porn stars do in the videos. Zoldbrod says they are in for a rude awakening when they have real-life sex.

In her book *What Are You Waiting For?* Dannah Gresh details a common delusion most young people have about pornography: they believe that their struggle with porn will go away once they're married. It's the number one topic engaged people ask about. As much as they hope their porn-addicted fiances will lose their online appetites, this is never true. Gresh writes:

> ...the lure of porn is never quenched by marital sex because porn has almost nothing to do with real love and real sex. It's as counterfeit as a counterfeit can be.

Similarly, author Nate Larkin shares that pornography corrodes relationships between men and women because lust kills love:

> Love gives; lust takes. Love sees a person; lust sees a body. Love is about you; lust is about me and my own gratification. Love seeks...knows...respects. Lust couldn't care less.

The bottom line is this: Porn satisfies lust, not love. Because lust is focused on self, it destroys relationships and love. The impacts of pornography can be devastating to relationships. Avoid it at all costs.

If you're already wrestling with addiction to porn, don't let shame keep you from seeking help. Consult a counselor as soon as possible to help you regain your freedom. Seek out a trusted pastor who will pray with you and walk beside you. Join a recovery group or friend group with others who share your struggle, who are fiercely committed to helping you grow and heal.

Questions for Reflection

1. How has porn impacted your life? How has this chapter opened your eyes to the damage it may be doing?

2. Think about your goals for sex in marriage. How will porn sabotage this vision, and hinder a healthy sex life?

3. What is one thing you can do today to protect yourself from porn? Who is one person you can talk to about your struggle?

CHAPTER 6

CARE OF THE SOUL

The Human Soul

Do you ever feel you're living two different lives—an outer life that everyone can see, and an inner life only you can see?

It's like living with a divided self. One side has an outer public life that everyone sees and uses to measure and judge us. Because it's visible, we try to manage this side especially well, so people think highly of us.

But we all have another side—a private inner life that we keep hidden from the rest of the world. We experience private struggles that nobody sees. We ask deep questions that others can't hear.

A lot of people try to approach God with their outer selves, in order to win His approval through performance, attractiveness, or behavior. I guess you could say that most of us share the same vision; unfortunately, it is the wrong vision. It is a vision based on how successful we can be in the visible, measurable dimensions of life. Over time we begin to realize that we are unable to make sense of all the struggles that we experience.

This is not the life that God intended for us. God wants us to be Christlike, which has nothing to do with outward performance or being religious. In fact, one of the problems with religion is that it does not touch and impact our hearts.

There are three characteristics of being Christlike.

1. The first has to do with your character.
2. The second has to do with the wisdom you possess.
3. The third has to do with your ability to love and to have deep, substantive relationships.

That's what being Christlike is all about.

Initially, I didn't find Christlikeness appealing, because I didn't have much of a view of Jesus at the time. This was in my early 20s, and I thought that Jesus was just a real religious guy—He didn't have a lot of fun, He didn't laugh much. But the more I studied His life, I realized that Jesus is *everything* that I would want to be.

The essence of true Christianity is the inner life—what God does in our souls. This is crucial to understand: every struggle originates in the soul. The soul is the very center of every human being. As Dallas Willard notes, at any given moment your soul is running your life. Willard says that the soul is *deep* in the sense of being basic or foundational but also in the sense that it lies almost totally beyond conscious awareness.

Those last words are significant: the soul "lies almost totally beyond conscious awareness." Because we are not fully aware of it, many of us neglect the importance of properly nurturing and caring for our souls. But neglecting our souls is dangerous. In 1 Peter 2:11, the apostle Peter warns us "to abstain from fleshly lusts which wage war against the soul."

In his wonderful book, *Soul Keeping,* John Ortberg shares a great story to illustrate the importance of protecting the soul:

There once was a town high in the Alps that straddled the banks of a beautiful stream. The stream was fed by springs that were as old as the earth and as deep as the sea.

The water was clear like crystal. Children laughed and played beside it; swans and geese swam on it. You could see the rocks and the sand and the rainbow trout that swarmed at the bottom of the stream.

High in the hills, far beyond anyone's sight, lived an old man who served as the Keeper of the Springs. He had been hired so long ago that now no one could remember a time when he wasn't there. He would travel from one spring to another in the hills, removing branches or fallen leaves or debris that might pollute the water. But his work was unseen.

One year the town council decided that they had better things to do with their money. No one supervised the old man anyway. They had roads to repair and taxes to collect and services to offer, and giving money to an unseen stream-cleaner had become a luxury that they could no longer afford.

So, the old man left his post. High in the mountains, the springs went untended; twigs, branches, and worse muddied the liquid flow. Mud and silt compacted the creek bed; farm wastes turned parts of the stream into stagnant bogs.

For a time, no one in the village noticed. But after a while, the water was not the same. It began to look brackish. The swans flew away to live elsewhere. The water no longer had a crisp scent that drew children to play by it. Some people in the town began to grow ill. All noticed the loss of sparkling beauty that fed the town. The life of the village depended on the stream, and the life of the stream depended on the keeper.

The city council reconvened, the money was found, and the old man was rehired. After yet another time, the springs were cleaned, the stream was pure, children played again on its banks, illness was replaced by good health, the swans came home, and the village came back to life. The life of the village depended on the health of the stream.

The stream is your soul. And you are the keeper.

I believe the best thing a person can do for the health of their soul is to stay close to and connected to Christ, the Good Shepherd. Though we're prone to wander from His presence, 1 Peter 2:25 reminds us: "For you were continually straying like sheep, but now you have returned to the Shepherd and Guardian of your souls."

Questions for Reflection

1. How often do you think about the fact that you have a soul? How does this change your perspective on life?

2. Why do you think people focus so much on their outer selves while neglecting their inner selves?

3. How do you stay connected to Christ? How would you like to become more connected to him?

The Thirst of the Soul

Sigmund Freud lived with a nagging longing within himself, which haunted him his whole life. This longing was a mystery to him, because he could never satisfy it. Freud never saw his unrest as a spiritual hunger, because he never believed in God or the human soul. But I believe that's *exactly* what he was experiencing. As Augustine writes: "You have made us for yourself, O Lord, and our heart is restless until it rests in you."

Psychiatrist Gerald C. May observed, "After twenty years of listening to the yearnings of people's hearts, I am convinced that human beings have an inborn desire for God. Whether we are consciously religious or not, this desire is our deepest longing and most precious treasure." The Bible describes this longing as a thirst of the soul. King David says, "For He has satisfied the thirsty soul, and the hungry soul He has filled with what is good." (Psalm 107:9)

As a counselor on our ministry staff said, "People are driven and ruled by unsatisfied desires, and they are desperately looking everywhere they can in hopes of finding satisfaction." Likewise, the prophet Jeremiah speaks of our fruitless quest for satisfaction:

For my people have committed two evils:
they have forsaken me,
   the fountain of living waters,
and hewed out cisterns for themselves,
      broken cisterns that can hold no water. (Jeremiah
2:13)

By looking for fulfillment apart from God, we forsake Him, the fountain of living waters. We construct our own cisterns, but the problem with self-made cisterns is that they leak. They can't hold water, leaving us *endlessly thirsty*. In the Gospel of John, Jesus declares, "If any man is thirsty, let him come to Me and drink. He who believes in Me, as the Scripture said, 'From his innermost being shall flow rivers of living water.'" (John 7:37-38)

Have you experienced the soul-quenching satisfaction of knowing Christ? Or have you been looking for satisfaction in things like academic success, popularity, athletic achievement, acceptance from a fraternity or sorority, attractiveness, sex, or influence? Only Christ will truly satisfy you.

C. S. Lewis brilliantly describes the soul's thirst for God in the *Chronicles of Narnia*, a series of allegorical children's stories, in which the powerful lion Aslan represents Christ. In one of the books, *The Silver Chair*, a young girl named Jill grows unbearably thirsty. She can hear a stream somewhere in the forest. Driven by her thirst, she begins to look for this source of water—cautiously, because she fears running into the Lion. She finds the stream, but is paralyzed by what she sees there: Aslan, huge and golden, still as a statue but terribly alive, is sitting beside the water. She waits for a long time, wrestling with her thoughts and hoping that he'll just go away. Then Aslan says, "If you are thirsty, you may drink." Jill is startled and refuses to come closer.

"Are you not thirsty?" said the Lion.

"I am dying of thirst," said Jill.

"Then drink," said the Lion.

"May I—could I—would you mind going away while I do?" said Jill.

The lion answered this only by a look and very low growl. And just as Jill gazed at its motionless hulk, she realized that she might as well have asked the whole mountain to move aside for her convenience.

The delicious rippling noise of the stream was driving her near frantic. "Will you promise not to—do anything to me, if I come?"

"I make no promise," said the Lion.

Jill was so thirsty now that, without noticing it, she had come a step nearer.

"Do you eat girls?" she said.

"I have swallowed up girls and boys, women and men, kings and emperors, cities and realms," said the Lion. It didn't say this as if it were boasting, nor as if it were sorry, nor as if it were angry. It just said it.

"I daren't come and drink," said Jill.

"Then you will die of thirst," said the Lion.

"Oh dear!" said Jill, coming another step nearer. "I suppose I must go and look for another stream then."

"There is no other stream," said the Lion.

So many people spend their lives looking for a stream to quench the thirsts of their souls. Jesus says *He* is that stream; apart from Him, satisfaction is impossible. He's very clear that if we refuse to drink from this spring—the fountain of living water—we will die. Without God, even the greatest college experience will leave you unsatisfied, so turn to Him, the one your soul was made for.

Questions for Reflection

1. Have you experienced the soul-satisfying wonder of knowing Christ? If yes, how can you deepen your relationship with Him? If not, what is holding you back from believing in Him?

2. As a college student, what are some common ways people seek satisfaction apart from Christ? Are you tempted by these things? How can you seek more satisfaction in Christ?

3. What is it about Jesus that makes Him all-satisfying? Why can He refresh your soul like nothing else can?

6.3
....

What's the Point of Life?

Several years ago, Nissan had a clever commercial that ended with the line, "Life is a journey, enjoy the ride." This initially seems to be a logical approach to life and, in fact, may be your approach. Life is a long, difficult journey, and you might as well enjoy yourself as much as possible, right?

We live in a world that encourages us to live in the moment, but sometimes at the expense of looking down the road. So ask yourself: Why are you here? What are your life goals? What kind of person do you want to be? What is your ultimate objective in life? And finally, when you reach the end of your life, what do you want to look back and see?

In Arthur Miller's Pulitzer Prize-winning play, *Death of a Salesman*, Willy Loman is a salesman who's been seeking business success all his life. One of his principal tactics is trying to impress others, always presenting himself as a big shot. Deep down, Loman is miserable. His family is dysfunctional. His career is actually a flop. Even on his best days, he is quite mediocre.

At the end of the play, Loman is fired from his job and faces the harsh reality of a disappointing life. He's been liv-

ing a charade, attempting to convince others he's successful. In the end, he takes his life.

Just after the funeral, Loman's wife asks their son Biff,
"Why did he do it? Why did he take his life?"

Biff responds, "He had the wrong dreams. All, all,
wrong. And he never knew who he was."

In these lines, Arthur Miller reveals the reality plaguing
so many people: they don't know who they are or where
they're going. They're slaves to the moment, driven along
by every wind of desire. If you ask them what the ultimate
object of life is, they have no idea.

In the biography of business icon Lee Iacocca, he reflects
on his life with these words: "Here I am in the twilight
years of my life, still wondering what it is all about. I can
tell you this, fame and fortune are for the birds." All his life,
Iacocca chased fame and fortune, but in his closing chapter
he regretted it. Don't make the mistake Iacocca did—think
deeply *today* about what your life is really about.

Nobel Prize-winning author Alexkandr Solzhenitsyn
provides some great insight into this issue. After writing
some negative remarks about Joseph Stalin, he spent eight
years in a Russian prison as punishment. He entered prison
as an atheist, but came out a committed Christian. Instead
of being angry and bitter about his imprisonment, the first
words out of his mouth about his prison experience were:
"I bless you, prison. I bless you for being in my life. For
there, lying on rotting prison straw, I learned the object of
life was not prosperity, as I had grown up believing, but is
the maturing of the soul."

Solzhenitsyn went into prison believing the universe
was godless and meaningless. He thought the object of life
was to be prosperous. However, his ideas about life were

transformed when he became a Christian. He realized the object of life involved his soul and its relationship to God. Solzhenitsyn discovered that, in Christ, life has purpose, and we don't have to spend our lives pursuing empty dreams.

College culture says to be impulsive, not intentional. Is your hope anchored in momentary success and pleasure, or the all-satisfying God who created you?

Questions for Reflection

1. What is your greatest goal in life? How did you arrive at this goal?

2. When you reach the end of your life, what do you hope people will say your life was about?

3. Have you allowed God (and the Bible) to shape your life goals? If not, how might your vision need to be reshaped?

Understanding Human Desire

When most people hear the word "wealth," they think of possessions: nice cars, big houses, and impressive bank accounts. But perhaps wealth is more than material things.

Miroslav Volf, a theologian at Yale Divinity School helpfully distinguishes between two types of wealth. He calls the first type "richness of having," which includes material possessions and financial assets. The second type of wealth is what he calls "richness of being," which involves our happiness and sense of well-being. Although many believe happiness comes from the richness of having, Volf says what we really long for is richness of being. We wrongly assume that more possessions will produce more happiness, but it never does. Why can't our stuff ultimately satisfy? It's because we are eternal beings, created by God with spiritual needs in our souls—needs that physical things can't quench.

Think about humanity's intangible cravings: joy, happiness, peace, and love (separate from sex). These are not physical desires of the body, but spiritual longings of the soul. Throughout the Bible, Scripture indicates that our souls have a thirst only God can quench. King David says: "My soul thirsts for God, for the living God." (Psalm 42:2)

When we attempt to satisfy our spiritual yearnings with physical things, it doesn't work. C.S. Lewis summarizes humanity's fruitless quest for happiness apart from God:

> Over the centuries men have tried to invent some sort of happiness for themselves outside of God, apart from God. And out of that hopeless attempt has come nearly all that we call human history—greed, poverty, selfish ambition, war, prostitution, classes, brutal empires, slavery—the long terrible story of man trying to find something other than God which will make him happy.

> The reason why it can never succeed in this: God made us, invented us as a man invents an engine. A car is made to run on gasoline, and it would not run properly on anything else. God designed humans to run on Himself. He Himself is the fuel our spirits were designed to burn, the food our spirits were designed to feed on. There is no other. That is why it is just no good asking God to make us happy in our own way, without bothering to have a relationship with Himself. God cannot give us happiness and peace apart from Himself, because it is not there. There is no such thing.

Augustine said: "If there is a God who brought us into existence, then the deepest chambers of our souls simply cannot be filled up by anything less than Him." Modern people, so wrapped up in consumerism and materialism, constantly struggle to find happiness, as Harvard psychologist Daniel Gilbert explains: "Most people do not know what will lead to their ultimate well-being, because our desires bear little relation to the things that truly make us happy." According to God, true wealth is about the contents of your soul, not your bank account.

Questions for Reflection

1. As you survey college life, where are most people seeking happiness? Where are you seeking happiness?

2. Why do you think so many people seek happiness in possessions? Why are possessions incapable of delivering long term happiness?

3. If a close relationship with God is the true definition of wealth, how are you "building your portfolio?" In other words, how are you growing closer to Him?

6.5

Finding Your Center

Are you a hedgehog or a fox?

In Isaiah Berlin's famous essay, "The Hedgehog and the Fox," he suggests that every person is one or the other. He writes:

> The fox knows many things, but the hedgehog knows one big thing. The fox is a cunning creature, able to devise a myriad of complex strategies for sneak attacks upon the hedgehog. Day in and day out, the fox circles around the hedgehog's den, waiting for the perfect moment to pounce. Fast, sleek, beautiful, fleet of foot, and crafty—the fox looks like the sure winner.
>
> The hedgehog, on the other hand, is a dowdier creature, looking like a genetic mix-up between a porcupine and a small armadillo. He waddles along, going about his simple day, searching for lunch and taking care of his home.
>
> The fox waits in cunning silence at the juncture in the trail. The hedgehog, minding his own business, wanders right into the path of the fox.
>
> "Aha, I've got you now!" thinks the fox. He leaps out, bounding across the ground, lightning fast. The

little hedgehog, sensing danger, looks up and thinks, "Here we go again. Will he ever learn?" Rolling up into a perfect little ball, the hedgehog becomes a sphere of sharp spikes, pointing outward in all directions. The fox, bounding toward his prey, sees the hedgehog's defense and calls off the attack. Retreating back to the forest, the fox begins to calculate a new line of attack. Each day, some version of this battle between the hedgehog and the fox takes place, and despite the greater cunning of the fox, the hedgehog always wins.

So which animal are you? Foxes chase individual pursuits without the big picture in mind. They are "scattered or diffused, moving on many levels," says Berlin, never integrating their thinking into one overall concept or unifying vision. Hedgehogs, on the other hand, simplify a complex world into a single organizing idea. For them, one basic principle unifies and guides everything. It doesn't matter how complex the world is; a hedgehog reduces all challenges and dilemmas to simple (indeed almost simplistic) ideas.

Princeton professor Marvin Bressler points out the power of the Hedgehog Concept: "You want to know what separates those who make the biggest impact from all the others who are just as smart? They're hedgehogs."

Do you have one thing at your core that unifies and guides everything in your life, like the hedgehog? Or are you scattered with no unifying vision, like the fox? I find that a majority of people today do not have a spiritual center in their lives and have no idea what they are living for. Consequently, life becomes complex and confusing, with no real sense of meaning.

Stephen Covey, in his best-selling book, *The 7 Habits of Highly Effective People,* says that every one of us has a "personal center." Whatever is at the center of our life will be the source of our security, guidance, wisdom, and power. For many, money becomes their center because they believe it can purchase everything their souls long for. Over time, however, they discover that money can't scratch the deepest itch in our soul.

As a college student, maybe the spontaneous fox sounds more fun than the predictable hedgehog. Fair enough. But those that persist in impulsiveness (like the fox) end up exhausted and far from their dreams. The hedgehog, over time, lives a far more fulfilling life. But that begs the question: what unifying principle is worthy of basing your whole life on?

Scripture teaches that God wants to be your center. He wants to guide you and walk beside you through these college years (and beyond). He wants to be your source of wisdom and security.

C.S. Lewis undeniably grasped this concept. He firmly believed that, until you make Christ your "personal center," life will remain aimless and hopeless. In his own search for spiritual truth, Lewis slowly came to believe in God. Eventually he came to realize that truth is not an abstract concept; it's a person whose name is Jesus. In Christ, C.S. Lewis found the one, single Person who could unify and guide his life. He found the very center from which all of life flows.

Questions for Reflection

1. Are you more like the hedgehog (focused) or the fox (scattered)?

2. Why do you think it's important to have a clear vision for your life? Have you identified that vision for yourself?

3. Have you made God the center of your life's vision? How can you place Him more at the center of your life?

The Modern Identity Crisis

In today's world, identity comes from success. It's easy to define yourself by what you do. But when a person's worth is primarily tied to accomplishments, the result is disastrous.

We saw this play out in a tragic way in the story of Kathy Ormsby. Ormsby was a pre-med honor student at North Carolina State University who held the collegiate record in the women's 10,000 meters. As a young runner, she had always dreamed of competing in the NCAA Track and Field Championship in Indianapolis, and at last, the day came. She was heavily favored to win her event.

But something unexpected happened during the race. Ormsby fell behind and was never able to catch the front runner. Right after she lost the race, she ran off the track, out of the stadium, to a nearby bridge where she shockingly jumped over the side. The forty-foot fall permanently paralyzed her from the waist down.

Her story hauntingly reminds us that when we base our worth in personal performance, we put our identities (and sometimes even our safety) at risk. Success is a shaky foundation to build your life on, because any perceived failure can deplete our sense of worth. How can we be delivered from this modern identity crisis?

Author Tim Keller tells a true story of two young men who attended his church in New York City. Both were exploring the Christian faith and also trying to build an acting career. As he tells this story, Keller refers to the men as Sam and Jim.

Sam was moving toward faith in Christ while Jim was moving away. As Jesus became more real to Sam, he stopped looking to his stage career as the measure of his worth. Then, Sam and Jim found themselves auditioning for the same role. It was a very big part in a very big production. If either of them had gotten the job, it would have propelled him to great heights.

So, they performed at the audition, but neither of them was chosen. They both were turned down. Jim, the one whom most people would have considered the more self-confident, was simply devastated, while Sam was just disappointed. Sam went out and got a job in business, and after that he kept one foot in acting. Over the years he became very active in the church and was reasonably successful in business.

Opportunities for stage and screen acting occurred occasionally, but he engaged in them only as an avocation. His life thrived. Jim, however, went into a tailspin. He was angry at himself and the industry and left acting altogether, but he hated any other job he took. He seldom remained in a job for more than a year, drifting from place to place.

What happened? Originally, both men had acting as the core of their identity. It was the main factor in their self-regard. But then Sam had an identity shift. Acting became a good thing but not an ultimate thing. His love of the stage was not evicted from his life, but its stranglehold on his self-image and worth was broken. It became part of who he was but not the essence of who he was. That's why the rejection of not getting the role could not get at his identity. It was safe, impervious, hidden in Jesus Christ.

Jim, however, had a highly vulnerable, modern identity. His failure was an ax blow to his psychological tree. The rejection went right to the root of what made him feel he counted, what made him significant.

This sobering story demonstrates how success-based identities can easily crush us, especially when things don't go our way. But we have the opportunity to break the world's hold on our lives by relinquishing our identities to Christ, allowing His love (not our accomplishments) to make us secure.

Each of us has to choose which god we're going to serve—then we have to live with the consequences that flow from that choice. This is the most important, life-defining decision we will ever make. Choose wisely! In Christ, there is no such thing as an identity crisis.

Questions for Reflection

1. What does it mean for a person to find their identity in Christ? How will that person react differently to good and bad experiences (compared to someone who seeks their identity in accomplishment or success)?

2. Are you tempted to find your identity more in what you do, rather than in Christ? If so, ask yourself, "What is my deep desire here? (acceptance, to prove my worth, earn love, etc. or other?) What steps can you take to anchor your identity more in Jesus?

3. Read through the following Bible passages, which all speak of identity in Christ. How can these verses inform how you view yourself? (John 1:12, 1 Corinthians 6:19-20, Galatians 3:27-28, Colossians 2:9-10; 3:1-3, 1 Peter 2:9)

4. Action Steps to Consider:

   • Network and fellowship with other Christians in your major, to encourage one another toward Christ, not self-exaltation.

   • Get to know older Christians in the vocation you're pursuing. Learn from their faith and wisdom.

   • Confess and release the ways you're seeking your identity in other things (like success, dating, sex, acceptance, wealth, fun experiences, etc).

The Rabbit That Won't Break Down

I f you achieved your greatest goal in life, do you think you'd be satisfied? The surprising truth is, probably not. I remember a wise old man once said, "The loneliest moment in life is when you have just experienced or achieved the ultimate, and it has let you down."

On May 30, 2019, Kyle Martin took the stage at his graduation ceremony to deliver his speech as valedictorian of The King's Academy preparatory school, an honor he'd worked furiously to achieve. But no one expected the raw honesty of his words that day:

I stand before you tonight as the 2019 valedictorian. This time last year, I found out that I was in the running for this title. It was then that I decided that I wanted it. So, I worked hard for it. I sacrificed for it and, yes, I stressed for it. And I got it! And, at our senior award ceremony, it felt so good when I heard my name announced with the title. So good! For about 15 seconds. Yeah. 15 seconds of my heart racing and my adrenaline pumping. 15 seconds of, "Yeah, I won!" 15 seconds of being at the top of the pile of all my accomplishments, and it felt euphoric. But there must come a 16th second. And, on that 16th second, I sat down on my seat, looked at my silver stole that says valedictorian, and I thought, "That's it? What just happened? Why am I not feeling anything else?"

To be honest, I don't even know what I was expecting. A parade of balloons to drop? Or maybe I was hoping that all my problems would fade away in comparison to this amazing achievement. But none of that happened, not even in my heart. I felt nothing. I was shocked.

Martin's words summarize the experience of many people, who rise to the top, only to find it doesn't deliver the euphoria or invincibility they hoped it would. Somewhere along the way, we've gone wrong in our search for satisfaction. We overestimate how long our positive emotional experience will last when we achieve our highest goals.

Philosopher Dallas Willard illustrated this concept with a true story of a dog race that took place in Florida:

> They train these dogs to chase an electric rabbit, and one night the rabbit broke down and the dogs caught it. But they didn't know what to do with it. They were just leaping around, yelping and biting one another, totally confused about what was happening. I think that's a picture of what happens to all sorts of people who catch the rabbit in their life. Whether it's wealth or fame or beauty or a bigger house, or whatever, the prize isn't what they thought it would be. And when they finally get it, they don't know what to do with their lives.

Willard believes this is why so many people are disappointed with life. The rabbit they chase does not satisfy. This is why he believed, "We all need a rabbit that won't break down." What fuels our lives must be something that transcends the individual life!

Tim Keller puts it in these words: "If you expect this world to give you happiness, you will be utterly disappointed, because you are asking the world to give you something it cannot give." As spiritual beings, our innermost desires can only be satisfied by God. God gave us the world to enjoy, but the world can never take his place in our lives.

This is why the Old Testament prophet Isaiah writes: "And the LORD will continually guide you, and satisfy your desire in scorched places, and give strength to your bones... you will be like a watered garden, and like a spring of water whose waters do not fail." (Isaiah 58:11)

I quoted Psychiatrist Gerald May earlier in the book, but it bears repeating here: "After 20 years of listening to the yearnings of people's hearts, I am convinced that human beings have an inborn desire for God. Whether we are consciously religious or not, this desire is our deepest longing and most precious treasure." This is the rabbit that won't break down.

Questions for Reflection

1. Have you ever achieved success, only to find it didn't make life more enjoyable? What did that experience teach you?

   ....

   ....

2. How do you think God defines success? How is His definition different from the world's definition?

   ....

   ....

3. How do you seek satisfaction in God? How might you seek more satisfaction in Him? Grab a friend and study these Bible passages together: Philippians 4:19, John 4:14; 6:35; 10:10, Jeremiah 31:25

_____
_____
_____
_____

CONCLUSION

OUR ULTIMATE GOOD

Follow the Right Map

You are what you love. That's the title of James Smith's fascinating book, which explains that we tend to love whatever we see as the "good life." Smith suggests it's impossible to *not* love—the heart is the "engine that drives our existence." So if you look at your primary patterns and habits, that is what you love. The best way to know what you *really* value is to look at what you're pursuing in life.

The problem is, we don't always love the right things. What are the "right things?" The Bible teaches that God should be our first love (Deuteronomy 6:5), and that we should orient everything in our lives around Him. This is how God designed us to function; like GPS on our phones, a life centered in God will always guide us to our desired destination (life with him). But when our longings are directed elsewhere, our GPS malfunctions. With false bearings, we end up lost. Smith writes:

> Our culture often sells us faulty, fantastical maps of "the good life" that paint alluring pictures that draw us toward them. All too often we stake the expedition of our lives on them, setting sail toward them with every sheet hoisted. And we do so without thinking about it because these maps work on our imagination, not our

intellect. It's not until we're shipwrecked that we realize we trusted faulty maps.

In his book, Smith calls this "misorientation." He shares
a great illustration, citing the account of a failed nine-
teenth-century polar expedition of the USS Jeannette, cap-
tained by Lieutenant George De Long. It's a cautionary tale
about the hazards of an inaccurate map. De Long's entire
expedition depended on incorrect maps of the North Pole.
Dr. August Petermann, who created the maps, suggested a
"thermometric gateway" through the ice that opened onto
a vast "polar sea" on the top of the world.

But that fair-weather passage did not exist. De Long's
entire expedition was based on a myth, ultimately putting
the whole crew in grave danger. As perilous ice quickly
surrounded the ship, reality set in. But it was too late. The
ship eventually sank as it was crushed by the ice. Of the 33
crew members on board, 20 perished, including De Long.

Most of us will never explore the arctic, but we all
have to navigate daily life. In his best-selling book, *The
Road Less Traveled*, Dr. Scott Peck says that our worldview
is our map—a map that will either lead us effectively or
disastrously:

> Our view of reality is like a map with which to nego-
> tiate the terrain of life. If the map is true and accurate,
> we will generally know where we are, and if we have
> decided where we want to go, we will generally know
> how to get there. If the map is false and inaccurate, we
> generally will be lost.

As you navigate college life, let God be your captain. Let His Word be your map. Let His Spirit be the wind in your sails. Though you will undoubtedly sail through dark, turbulent waters from time to time, He will guide you safely to your destination.

Questions for Reflection

1. How accurate is your map (worldview)? Who or what has influenced your view of reality? Is your map drawn from the truth of God's Word, or some less reliable source? How is that map working for you?

2. What are you pursuing most passionately right now, and what does that say about your priorities?

3. How do you want God to guide you through your college experience? Write out a prayer to God, expressing your gratitude to Him, as well as your requests for Him to guide you.

What Has Happened
at Harvard?

If you ask most college students what the most prestigious university in America is, they're likely to say Harvard (no offense to all other fine institutions out there).

Harvard was founded in 1636. Most people don't know that Harvard's original mission statement read:

> Let every student be plainly instructed and earnestly pressed to consider well the end of his life and studies is to know God and Jesus Christ, which is eternal life, and therefore to lay Christ in the bottom, as the only foundation of all sound knowledge and learning.

As this mission statement indicates, for many years Harvard was a spiritually vibrant place. In fact, many would say this is what led to its initial greatness as an educational institution.

But today, it seems like Jesus has been expelled from the institution. In 1985, when Henri Nouwen resigned from Harvard Divinity School, he described the place as a "spiritual desert." To him, it seemed that God was dead at Harvard, even at the divinity school.

In February of 1993, Billy Graham had a lengthy meeting with Harvard's president, Derek Bok. As he was leaving, he asked Bok a final question: "What is the number one struggle Harvard students have to contend with?" Bok immediately responded, "Living with emptiness."

Kelly Kullberg, one of the chaplains of Harvard Graduate School Christian Fellowship, founded the Veritas Forum at Harvard where students could find community and ask hard questions about faith. Upon hearing the response Dr. Bok gave to Billy Graham, she asked this question: "How did such a great institution like Harvard become a place of emptiness?"

Kullberg encountered a particularly devastating situation as she worked to minister to some of the women at Harvard Divinity School. She attended a meeting that was held in the University Chapel. The meeting was for women only and was called the "Full Moon Circle." The group described themselves as a Neo-pagan, pre-Christian, Eco-feminist Wiccan Society. Kullberg says the chapel was packed and the women chanted to spirits, worshiped the full moon and attempted to reach their dead ancestors. She says it was shocking to see these bright, educated women acting as if they were unenlightened pagans.

In 2004, the cover story of the student newspaper, "The Crimson," revealed the pervasiveness of student depression on campus. The newspaper reported that, of the 6,700 undergraduate students enrolled, 80% had experienced depression at least once during the school year. Almost half (47%) of the student body found themselves depressed to the point of having difficulty functioning, and 650 students (10%) had strongly considered committing suicide.

Tomas Masaryk, the first president of liberated Czechoslovakia after World War I, wrote a book entitled *Suicide and the Meaning of Civilization*. His thesis is that the more godless a society becomes, the more its suicide rate increases. His research indicates that in the middle ages, the number of suicides was negligible. However, by the end of the nineteenth century, suicide was a leading cause of death. Today, suicide has surpassed car crashes as the leading cause of death due to injury. According to Masaryk's findings, the majority of suicides occur among well-educated people who consider themselves nonreligious. His conclusion reveals the tragic reality that people without faith feel they have no reason to live.

Dr. Armand Nicholi was a professor of psychiatry at Harvard Medical School, who also taught a popular undergraduate course there for 35 years. He routinely asked his undergraduate students if they (and the people around them) were happy. Invariably they answered, "No." When asked why, they generally responded that their lives and relationships lacked meaning.

In order to find meaning, you must look to God to answer the significant questions of life. College is an ideal time to consider your purpose in the world. So many people have moved away from the Biblical worldview that has always supplied the answers to these questions. But the questions remain, and the only way to find peace with these questions is to return to the source of all knowledge and truth: God Himself.

Questions for Reflection

1. Why do you think so many college students suffer from depression?

   _____

   _____

2. Based on Masaryk's research, why do you think nonreligious people experience a higher rate of depression?

   _____

   _____

3. As a Christian (if you are one), how might God use you to encourage and strengthen others on your college campus?

   _____

   _____

A Final Challenge

I hope you have found this book encouraging and helpful to your college journey. As we wrap up, I'd like to leave you with a challenge. In one of my favorite films, *Dead Poets Society*, there is a powerful scene that has deeply moved me since the first time I saw it over 30 years ago.

It's the first day of class at Welton Academy, a prestigious prep school for young men. Welton is steeped in history and tradition. Mr. Keating, a new English teacher (played by Robin Williams), calls the class to order. Unexpectedly, he takes the class out into the hall to look at some old black-and-white photos enclosed in trophy cases lining the walls. In the photos are young men who attended Welton more than half a century earlier. Mr. Keating says to his students:

We are food for worms. Believe it or not, each and every one of us in this room is one day going to stop breathing, turn cold, and die. I would like you to peruse some of the faces from the past. You've walked by them many times, but I don't think you've really looked at them.

They're not that different from you, are they? Same haircuts. Full of hormones, just like you. Invincible, just like you feel. The world is their oyster. They believe they are destined for great things, just like many of you. Their eyes are full of hope, just like you. Did they wait until it was too late to make from their lives even one iota of what they were capable of? Because you see, gentlemen, these boys are now fertilizing daffodils. If you listen real close you can hear them whisper their legacy to you. Go on, lean in. Do you hear it?

As the boys curiously lean in toward the glass case, Professor Keating whispers in their ears, "Car-pe, car-pe, carpe diem. Seize the day, boys! Make your lives extraordinary!"

Then, he leaves them with these powerful words: "Since your destiny is yet to be determined, why not make it extraordinary and leave a lasting legacy?"

Mr. Keating recognizes a classic human flaw: We are, by nature, short-term in our thinking. So he presents these young men with a powerful challenge: *What do you want your life to have been about when you get to the end of it?* He tries to give them a longer-term perspective, so they'll make the most of the time they have.

So, I leave you with the same challenge Mr. Keating gave his students:

"Since your destiny is yet to be determined, why not make it extraordinary and leave a lasting legacy?"

Sources

1. WISDOM FOR THE JOURNEY

1.1 The Path of Wisdom

Light, Richard, Dr., "How to Live Wisely", *The New York Times*, July 31, 2015.

Covey, Stephen R., *The Seven Habits of Highly Effective People: Restoring the Character Ethic,* Fireside Books: Simon and Schuster, New York, 1989.

Pascal, Blaise, and W F. Trotter. *Pascal's Pensées.* J.M. Dent & Sons, London, 1931.

1.2 The Value of Wisdom

Proverbs 27:12, New American Standard Bible.

Stanley, Andy. *The Principle Of The Path,* Thomas Nelson, Nashville, TN, 2008.

Wolfe, Tom, "The Great Relearning - 20th Century is Over", *The American Spectator,* Arlington, Virginia, December 1987.

Ecclesiastes 7:12.

1.3 The Key to a Healthy Life

Dr. Scott Peck, *The Road Less Traveled,* Simon and Schuster, New York, 1978.

Peterson, Jordan, *12 Rules for Life,* Random House Canada, Toronto, 2018.

Kent, Jack, *There's No Such Thing as a Dragon,* Golden Book, New York, 2005.

2. LIVING AN EXCEPTIONAL LIFE

2.1 The Life That Could Have Been

Wilde, Oscar, and Ross, Robert Baldwin, *De Profundis*, Methuen and Co., London, 1905.

Harris, Alex and Harris, Brett, "Do Hard Things", Multnomah, Colorado Springs, CO, 2016.

John Piper, Think: *The Life of the Mind and the Love of God*, Crossway, Wheaton, Ill., 2011.

2.2 The Art of Achieving

Seligman, Dr. Martin, *Flourish*, Free Press, New York, 2012.

2.3 Disordered Priorities

Buford, Bob, (Dr. Armand Nicholi, as quoted in) *Finishing Well*, Zondervan, Grand Rapids, Mich., 2011.

Lewis, C.S., "The Inner Ring," speech at King's College, University of London, London, 1944.

2.4 Understanding Our Habits

Morris, Dr. Tom, *Plato's Lemonade Stand*, Wisdom/Works, 2019.

Clear, James, *Atomic Habits*, Random House, New York, 2018.

2.5 The Power of Discipline

Proverbs 25:28.

Stanley, Andy, *How to Be Rich: It's Not What You Have. It's What You Do With What You Have*, Zondervan, Grand Rapids, Mich., 2013.

Magazine article, "Discipline," Source Unknown.

2.6 The Daffodil Principle

Stanley, Andy, *The Best Question Ever*, Multnomah, Colorado Springs, CO, 2004.

Einstein, Albert, https://quotesonfinance.com/quote/79/albert-einstein-compound-interest

Hardy, Darren, *The Compound Effect*, Vanguard Press: Perseus Books Group, Philadelphia, PA, 2010.

Edwards, Jaroldeen, *The Daffodil Principle,* Salt Lake City, UT: Deseret Book Co., 2004.

3. WHAT IS TRUE FREEDOM?

3.1 Freedom and the Control of Our Desires
John 10:10.

3.2 Freedom Without Restrictions
Durkheim, Émile, Suicide: *A Study in Sociology,* Trans. Spaulding, John A., The Free Press, New York, 1979 (1897).

3.3 Freedom and the Pursuit of Happiness
Yancey, Philip, *Soul Survivor: How Thirteen Unlikely Mentors Helped My Faith Survive the Church,* Doubleday, New York, 2003.
James 1:25.
Keller, Tim, *Preaching: Communicating Faith in an Age of Skepticism,* Penguin Publishing Group, New York, 2015.

4. PRINCIPLES TO FOLLOW

4.1 Social Intelligence
The Wall Street Journal, Article Title Unknown.
Hyatt, Carole, and Gottlieb, Linda, *When Smart People Fail,* Simon and Schuster, New York, NY, 1987.
Ryle, John Charles (J.C.), *Expository Thoughts on the Gospels,* R. Carter & Brothers, New York, 1860.
Carnegie Foundation for the Advancement of Teaching, *A Study of Engineering Education,* authored by Charles Riborg Mann and published in 1918 by the Carnegie Foundation, pages 106-107.
Carnegie, Dale, *How To Win Friends And Influence People,* Simon & Schuster, New York, 1936.
Rockefeller, John D., https://www.brainyquote.com/quotes/john_d_rockefeller_147467.
Maxwell, John, *Failing Forward: Turning Mistakes into Stepping Stones*

for Success, Thomas Nelson, Nashville, TN, 2007.

4.2 Be a Student for Life

Munger, Charlie, "Prescriptions for Misery", Harvard commencement address, Boston, MA, June 13, 1986.

"Alabama mans 20-mile walk to work attracts praise, new car", The Pelham Reporter, July 16, 2018,

https://www.thereporter.com/2018/07/16/alabama-mans-20-mile-walk-to-work-attracts-praise-new-car

4.3 The Progress Paradox

Ashbery, John, "Why We Feel So Bad When We Have It So Good", *Forbes Magazine,* Jersey City, NJ, September 14, 1992.

Swenson, Dr. Richard, *Margin,* NavPress, Colorado Springs, CO, 2004.

4.4 Decisions and Choices

Guinness, Os, *The Call,* Thomas Nelson: Word Publishing, Nashville, TN, 1998.

Isaiah 3:10.

Psalm 7:15.

Lewis, C.S., *Mere Christianity,* Macmillan, New York, NY, 1960.

Will, Mike, Douglas Davis, Pierre Ramon Slaughter, Timothy Thomas, Theron Thomas, and Ricky Walters, "We Can't Stop", (Recorded by Miley Cyrus, Album "Bangerz"), RCA Records, 2013.

Chris Thurman, *The Lies We Believe,* Thomas Nelson, Nashville, TN, 2003.

Hall, Mark, *Slow Fade,* (Recorded by Casting Crowns, Album "The Altar and the Door"), Beach Street Records / Reunion Records, 2007.

4.5 A Prescription for Misery

Friedman, Thomas, "How to Get a Job at Google", *The New York Times,* Feb. 22, 2014.

Holiday, Ryan, *Ego is the Enemy,* Portfolio: Penguin Books, New York, 2016.

Munger, Charlie, USC Gould School of Law commencement address, Los Angeles, CA, May 13, 2007.

Senator John Danforth, Katharine Graham eulogy, Washington National Cathedral, Jul 23, 2001, https://cathedral.org/sermons/homily/

Williams, Pat, *Humility*, (quote by Dr. Sheila Murray Bethel), Shiloh Run Press: Barbour Publishing, Uhrichsville, OH, 2016.

5. HUMAN SEXUALITY

5.1 Are There Any Rules for Sex

Jordan Peterson, *Hookup Culture & Consent.* https://www.youtube.com/watch?v=duBRl0gRBDs (no longer available on YouTube), 2019.

Leonard, George, *The End of Sex: Erotic Love after the Sexual Revolution*, J.P. Tarcher, Distributed by Houghton Mifflin, Boston, MA, 1983.

Ray Ortlund, https://sermonquotes.com/ray-ortlund-2/12795-sex-is-like-fire-in-the-fireplace-it-keeps-us-warm-outside-the-fireplace-it-ray-ortlund.html

Matthew 19:4-5.

Genesis 2:24.

Philip Yancey, *What Good Is God?: In Search of a Faith That Matters*, FaithWords: Hachette Book Group, New York, NY, 2010.

5.2 Sex and the Pursuit of Happiness

Freud, Sigmund, David McLintock, and Sigmund Freud, *Civilization and Its Discontents*, Penguin, London, 2002.

Isaiah 5:20.

David F. Wells, *Losing Our Virtue: Why the Church Must Recover Its Moral Vision*, Eerdmans, Grand Rapids, MI, 1999.

Elisabeth Elliot, *Passion and Purity: Learning to Bring Your Love Life Under Christ's Control*, Revell Books: Baker Publishing Group, Ada, MI, 1984.

5.3 The Beauty of Discovery

Naomi Wolf as quoted in April Witt, "Blog Interrupted," The Washington Post Magazine, August 15, 2004, 16.

Ecclesiastes 7:8.

Stedman, Ray, "Whoever said Life was Fair?", Series: Things that Don't Work: Ecclesiastes, Ray Stedman Ministries, October 31, 1982

Swindoll, Charles, *Strike the Original Match*, Zondervan, Grand Rapids, MI, 1993.

Unwin, Joseph Daniel (J.D.), *Sex and Culture*, Oxford University Press, London, 1934.

5.4 How to Ruin Your Sex Life

Maltz, Wendy and Larry, *The Porn Trap*, HarperCollins Publishers, New York, 2008.

Wolf, Naomi, "The Porn Myth", *New York Magazine*, October 20, 2003.

Ofman, Dr. Ursula, "Internet Porn", *New York Magazine*, October 10, 2003.

Paul, Pamela, *Pornified*, Henry Holt & Co., New York, NY, 2006.

Zoldbrod, Aline, as quoted in *Pornified*, by Pamela Paul, Henry Holt & Co., New York, NY, 2006.

Gresh, Dannah, *What Are You Waiting For? The One Thing No One Ever Tells You About Sex*, WaterBrook Press, Colorado Springs, CO, 2011.

Larkin, Nate, *Samson and the Pirate Monks*, Thomas Nelson, Nashville, TN, 2007.

6. CARE OF THE SOUL

6.1 The Human Soul

Ortberg, John, *Soul Keeping*, Zondervan, Grand Rapids, MI, 2014.

I Peter 2:25.

6.2 The Thirst of the Soul

Augustine, of Hippo, Saint, and Warner, Rex. *The Confessions of St. Augustine*, Penguin Group, New York, 1981.

May, Gerald G., *Addiction and Grace*, HarperSanFrancisco, San Francisco, CA, 1988.

Psalm 107:9.

Jeremiah 2:13.

John 7:37-38.

Lewis, C.S., *The Chronicles of Narnia: The Silver Chair*, HarperCollins, New York, NY, 2005 (first published September 7th 1953).

6.3 What's the Point of Life?

Miller, Arthur. *Death of a Salesman*, Penguin Modern Classics, London, 1996.

Iacocca, Lee, *Lee Iacocca: An Autobiography*, Bantam, New York, NY, 1986.

Solzhenitsyn, Aleksandr, *Gulag Archipelago II*, Harper and Row, New York, NY, 1974.

6.4 Understanding Human Desire

Volf, Miroslav as quoted in *When the Game Is Over, It All Goes Back in the Box*, John Ortberg, Zondervan, Grand Rapids, MI, 2007.

Psalm 42:2.

Lewis, C.S., *Mere Christianity*, Macmillan, New York, NY, 1960.

Gilbert, Daniel, *Stumbling on Happiness*, Alfred A. Knopf: Random House Books, New York, NY, 2006.

6.5 Finding Your Center

Berlin, Isaiah. 1953. *The hedgehog and the fox; an essay on Tolstoy's view of history*, Simon & Schuster, New York, NY, 1953.

Bressler, Marvin, as quoted in *Good to Great: Why Some Companies Make the Leap and Others Don't*, by Jim Collins, HarperCollins Publishers, Harper Business, New York, NY, 2001.

Covey, Stephen R., *The Seven Habits of Highly Effective People: Restoring the Character Ethic*, Fireside Books: Simon and Schuster, New York, NY, 1989.

Lewis, C.S., *Mere Christianity*, Macmillan, New York, NY, 1960.

6.6 The Modern Identity

Keller, Tim, *Making Sense of God: Finding God in the Modern World*, Penguin, New York, NY, 2016.

6.7 The Rabbit That Won't Break Down

Martin, Kyle, valedictory address at Kings Academy Prep school in West Palm Beach, Florida, May 30th, 2019, https://www.youtube.com/watch?v=T76FdtKreNQ

Willard, Dallas, *Renovation of the Heart: Putting on the Character of Christ*. NavPress, Colorado Springs, CO, 2002.

Keller, Tim, *Hope in Times of Fear*, Penguin, New York, NY, 2021.

Isaiah 58:11.

May, Gerald G., *Addiction and Grace*, HarperSanFrancisco, San Francisco, CA, 1988.

CONCLUSION: OUR ULTIMATE GOOD

Follow the Right Map

Smith, James K.A., *You Are What You Love*, Brazos Press: Baker Publishing Group, Grand Rapids, MI, 2016.

Deuteronomy 6:5.

Dr. Scott Peck, *The Road Less Traveled*, Simon and Schuster, New York, NY, 1978.

What Has Happened at Harvard?

Esteller, Juan V., "The Secular Life at Harvard", *The Harvard Crimson*, January 19, 2016, https://www.thecrimson.com/article/2016/1/19/secular-harvard-esteller/

Kullberg, Kelly Monroe, *Finding God Beyond Harvard*, IVP Books, Downers Grove, Ill., 2006.

Masaryk, Tomas, *Suicide and the Meaning of Civilization*, Univ. of Chicago Press, Chicago, Ill., 1970.

A Final Challenge

Weir, Peter, Steven Haft, Paul Junger Witt, Tony Thomas, Tom Schulman, Robin Williams, Robert Sean Leonard, et al., *Dead Poets Society*, Buena Vista Pictures Distribution: Touchstone Home Video, Burbank, CA, 1998.